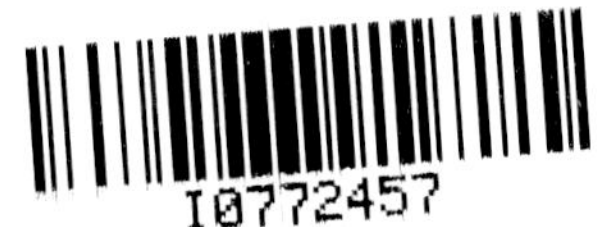

cute kawaii coloring book

F. FRANKLIN

Testing page

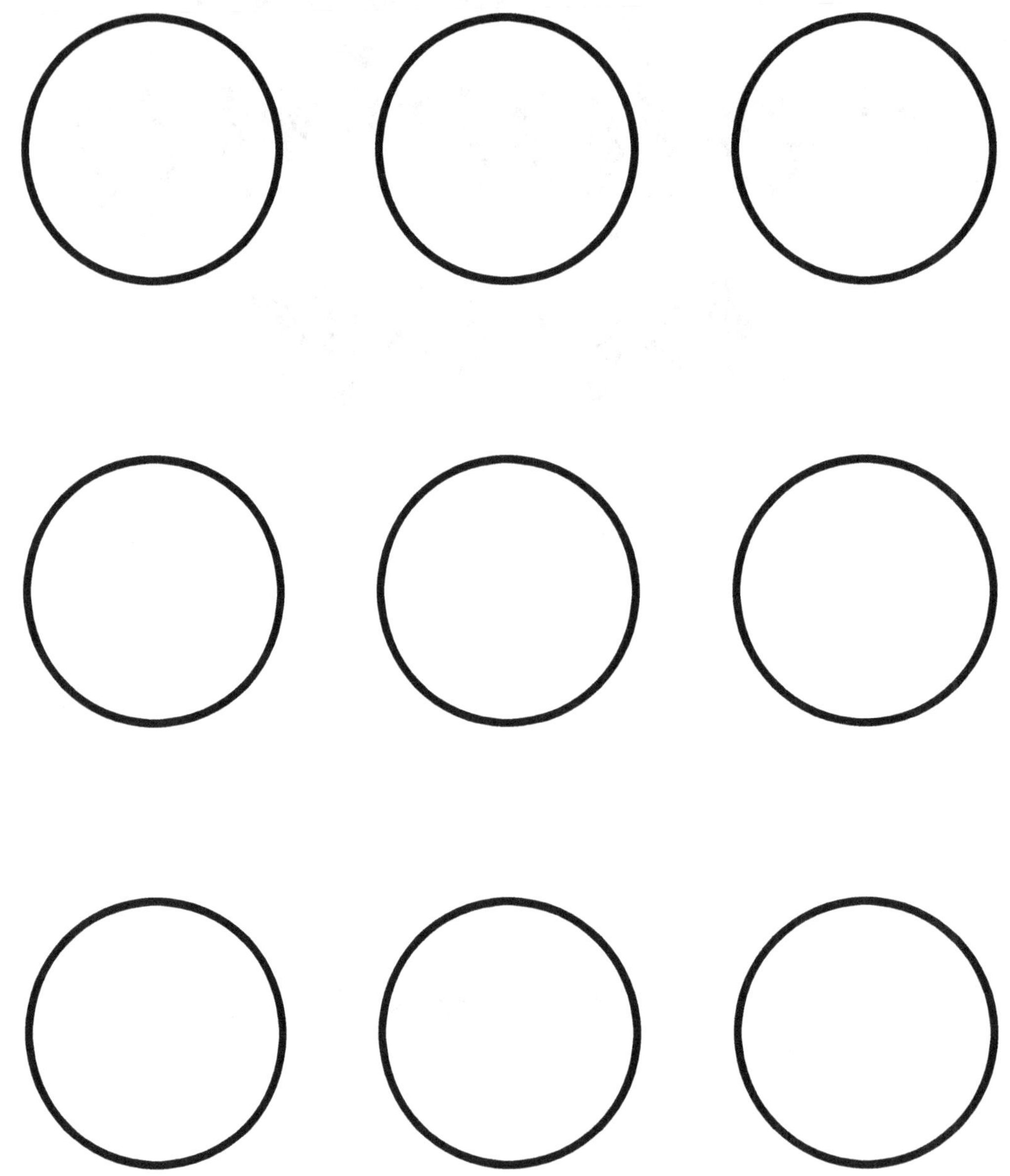

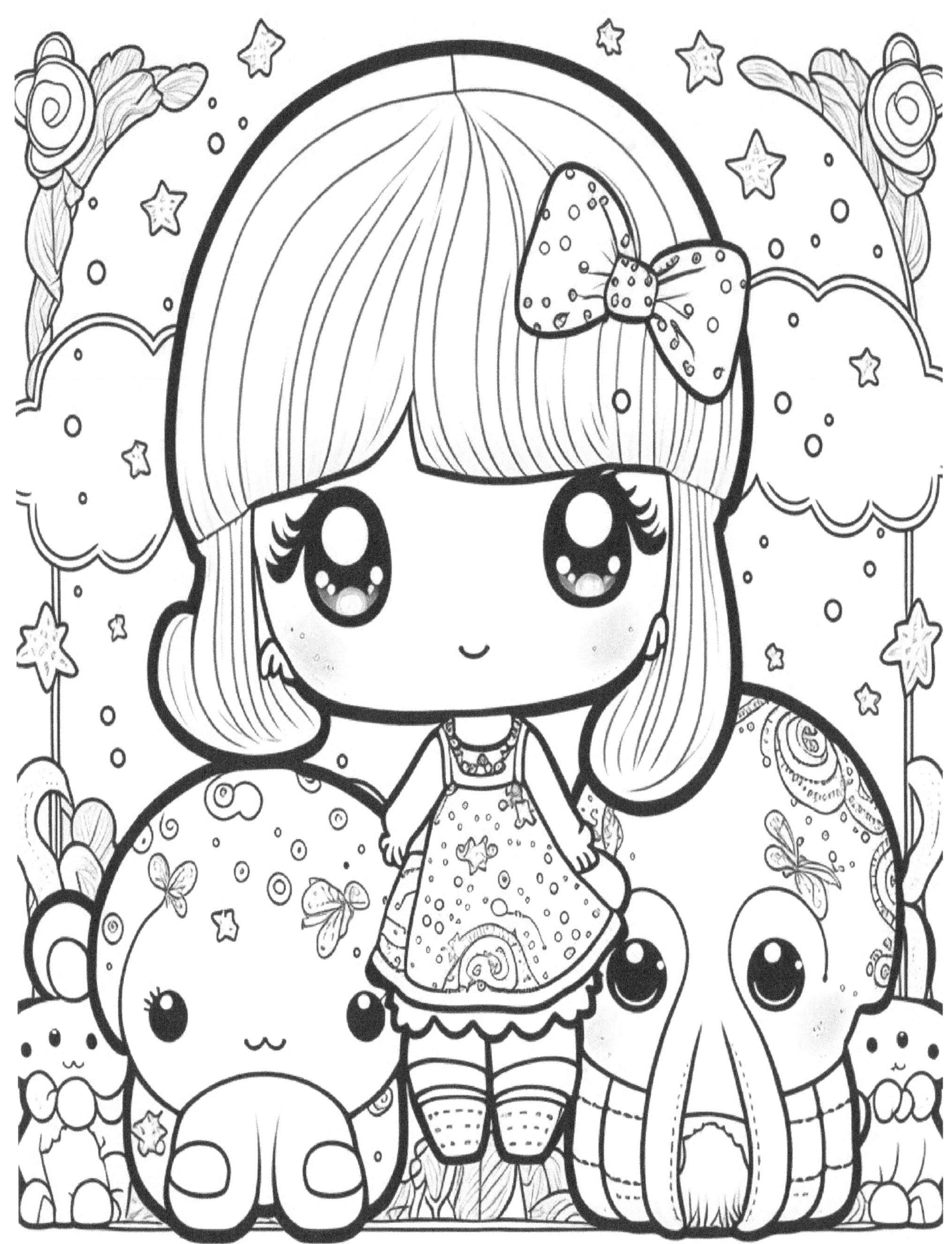

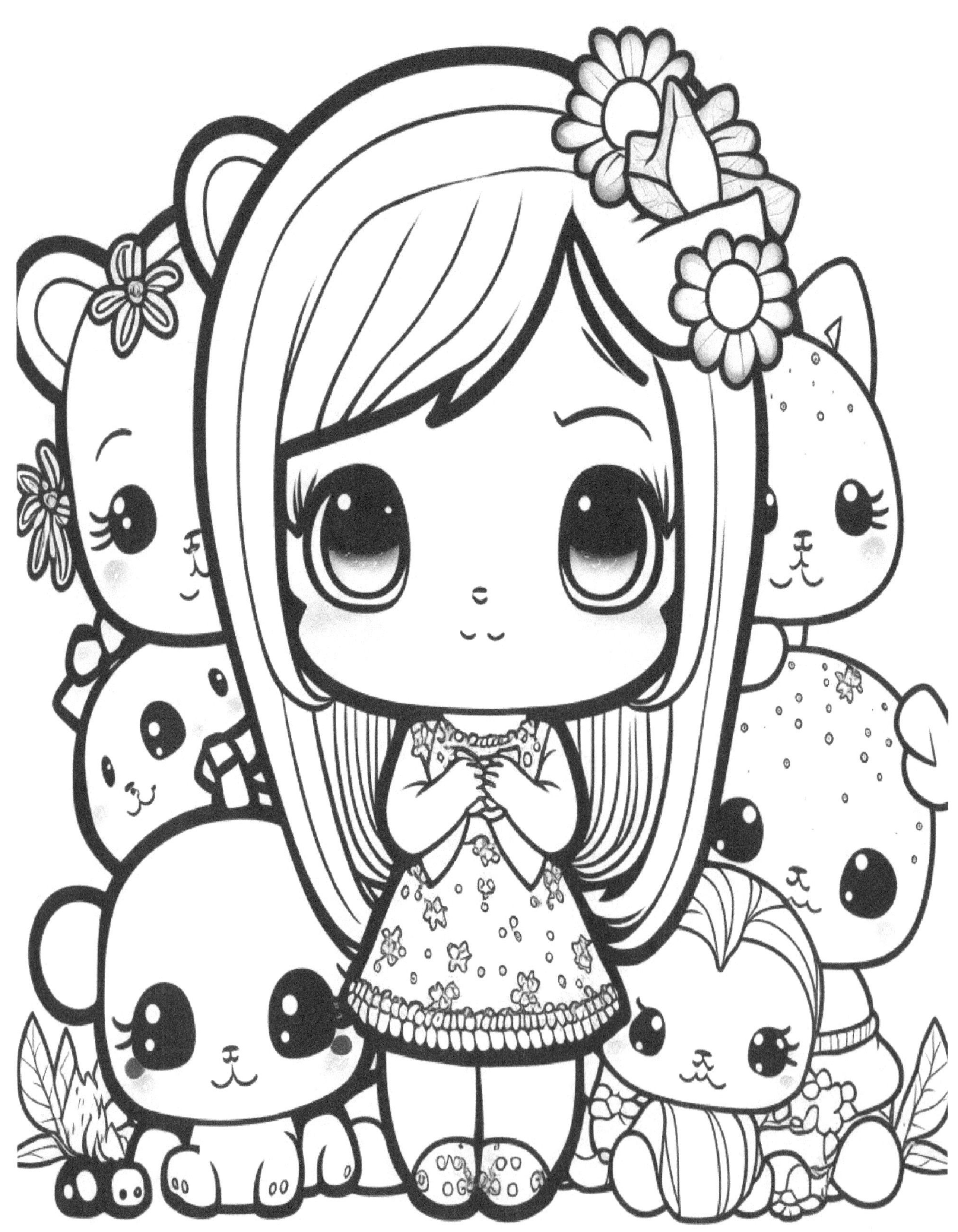

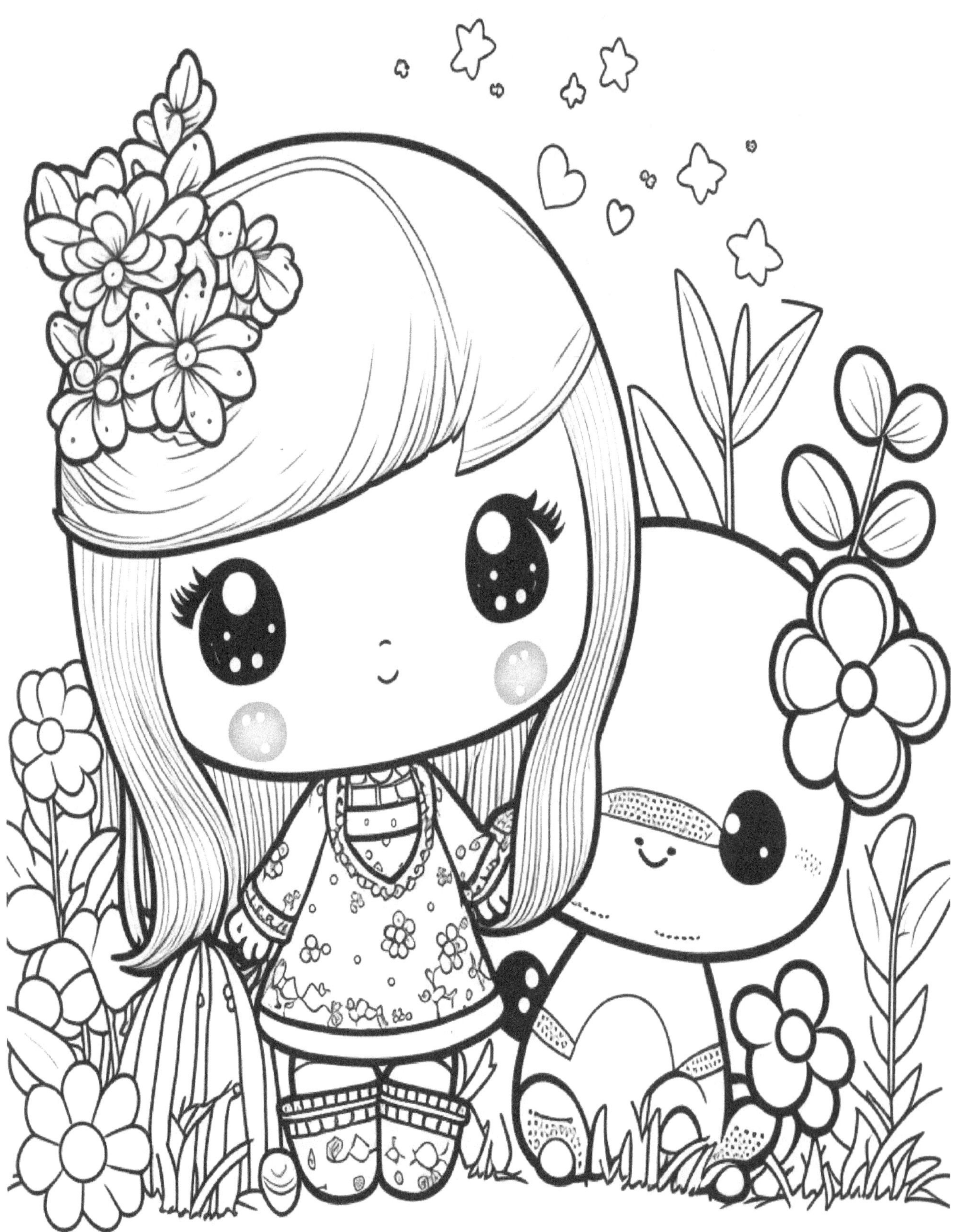

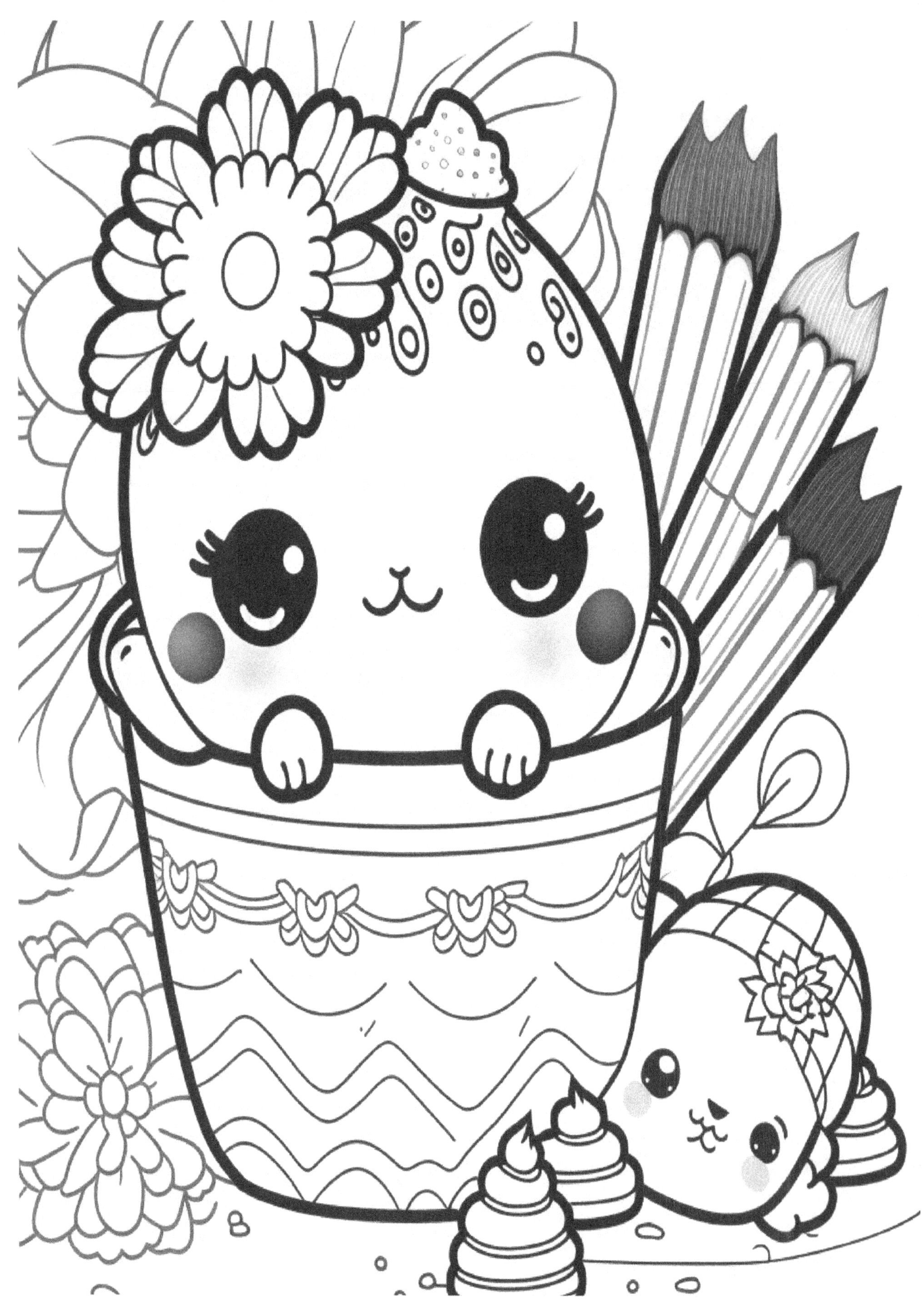

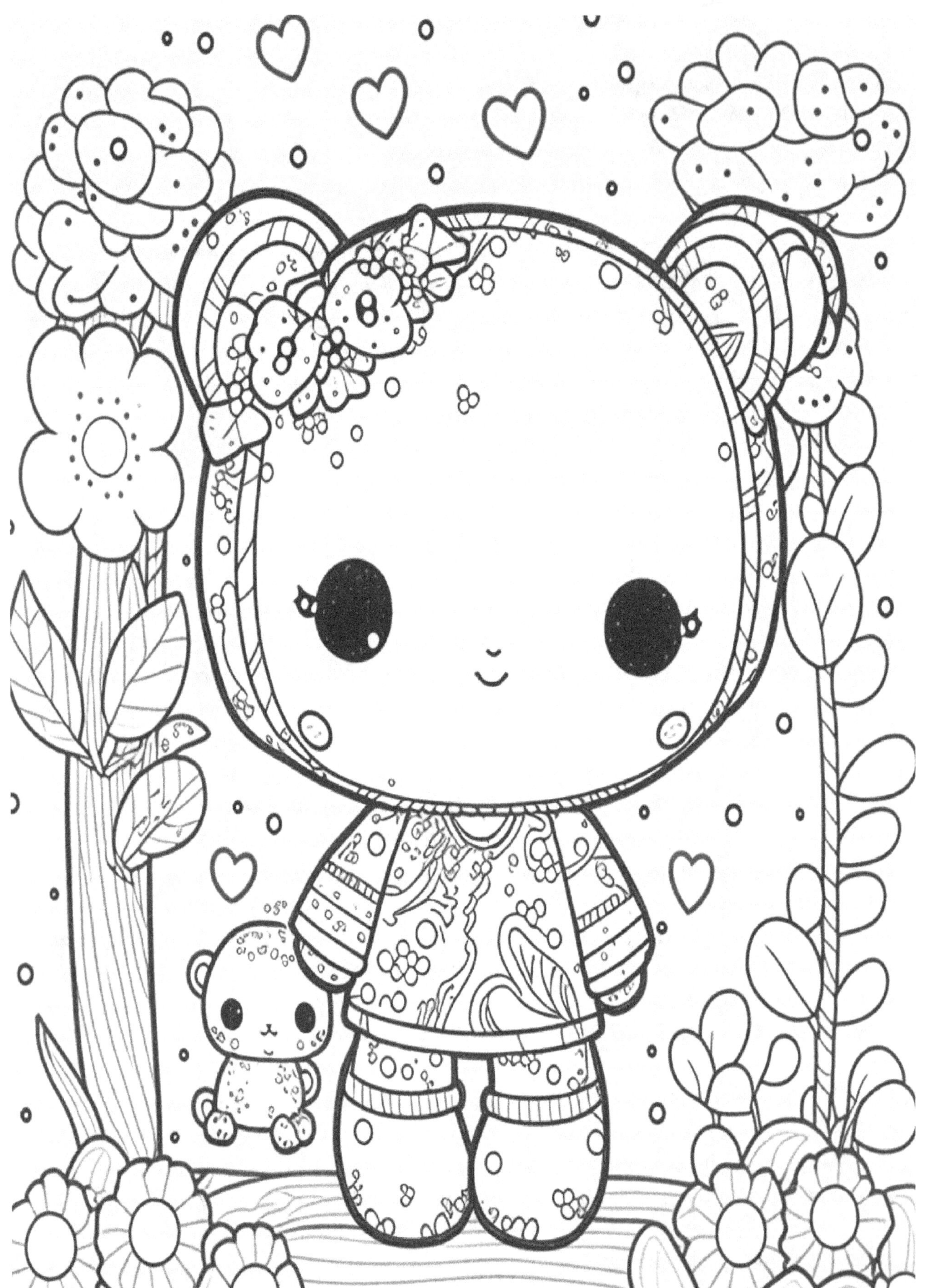

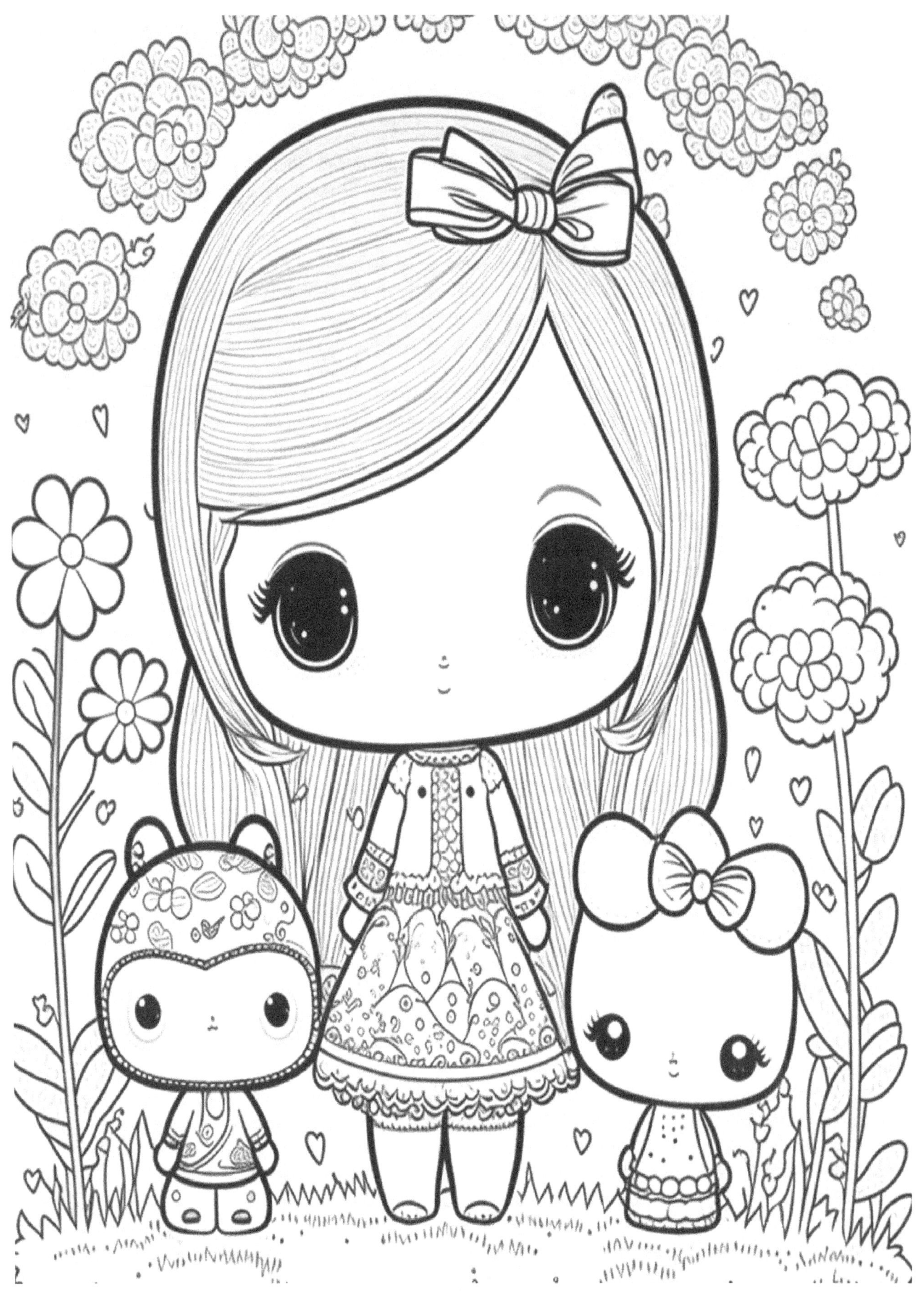

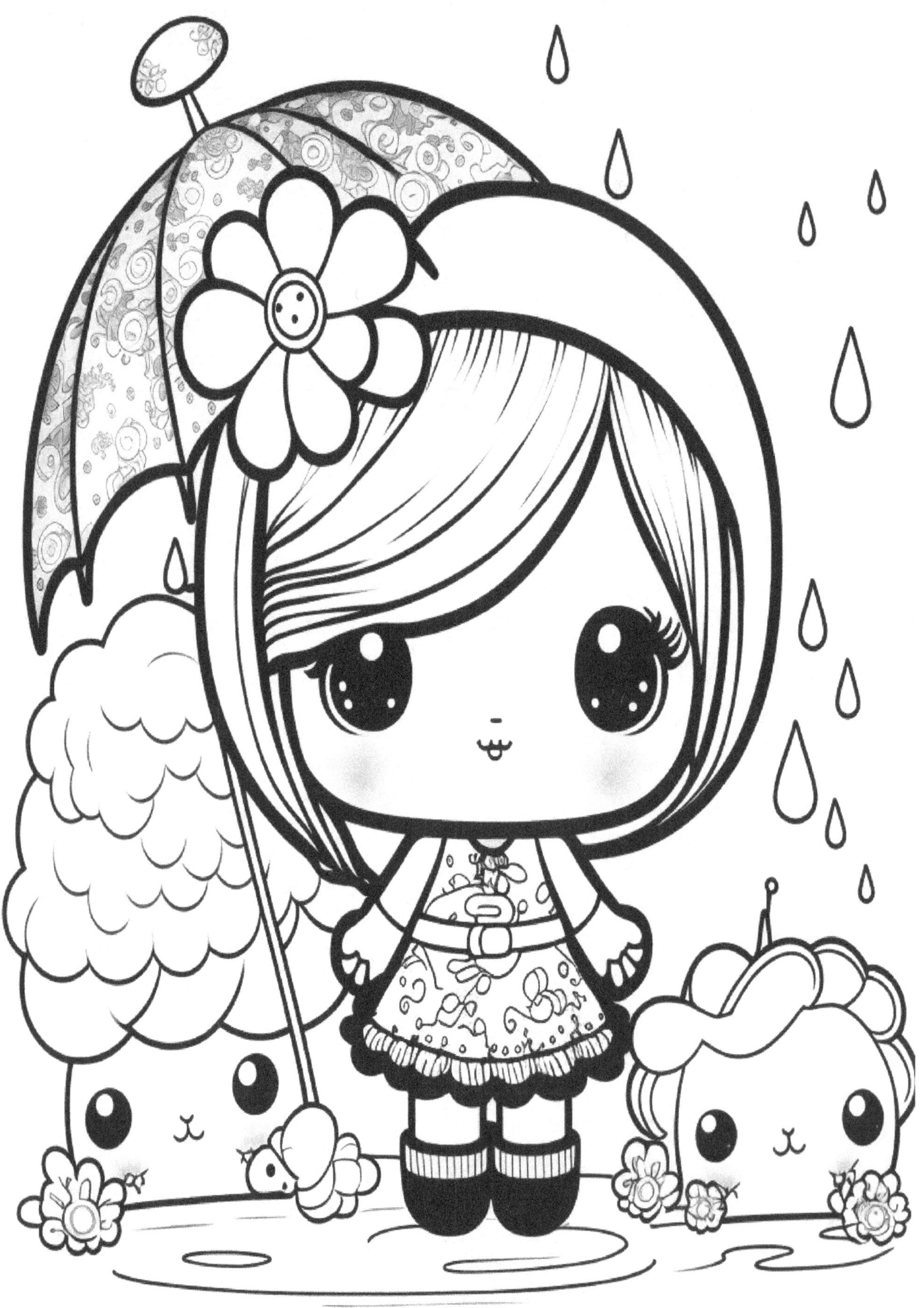

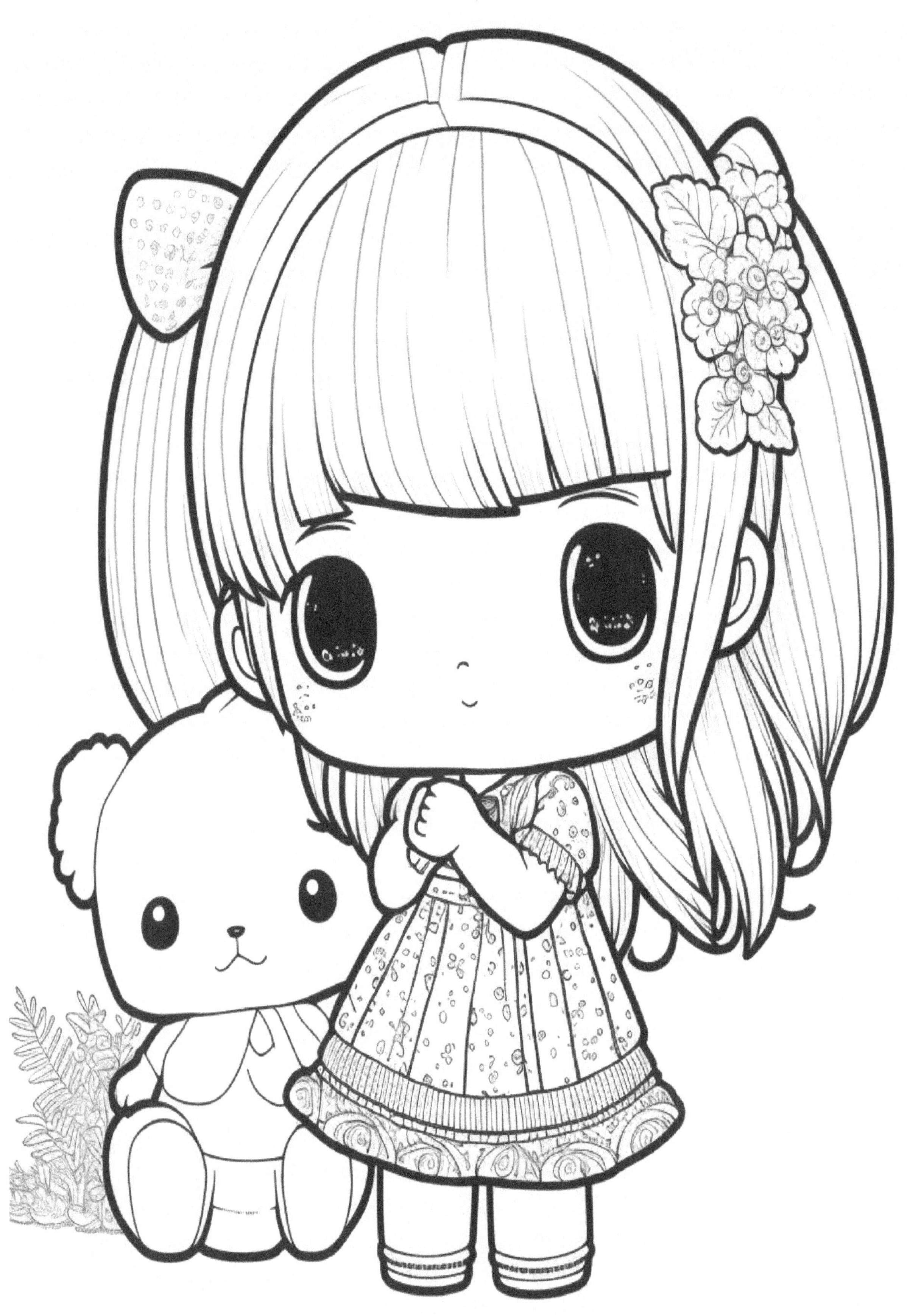

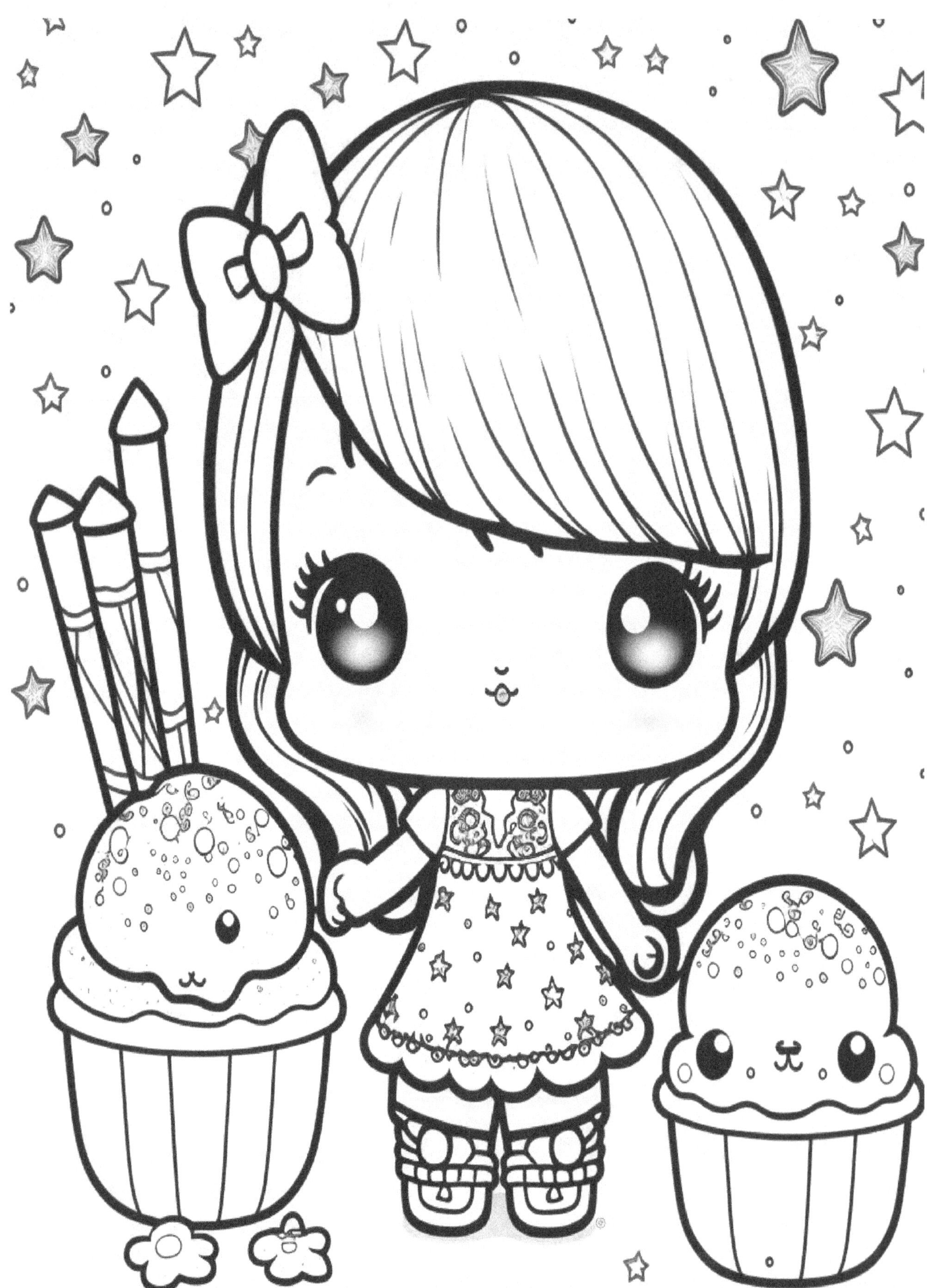

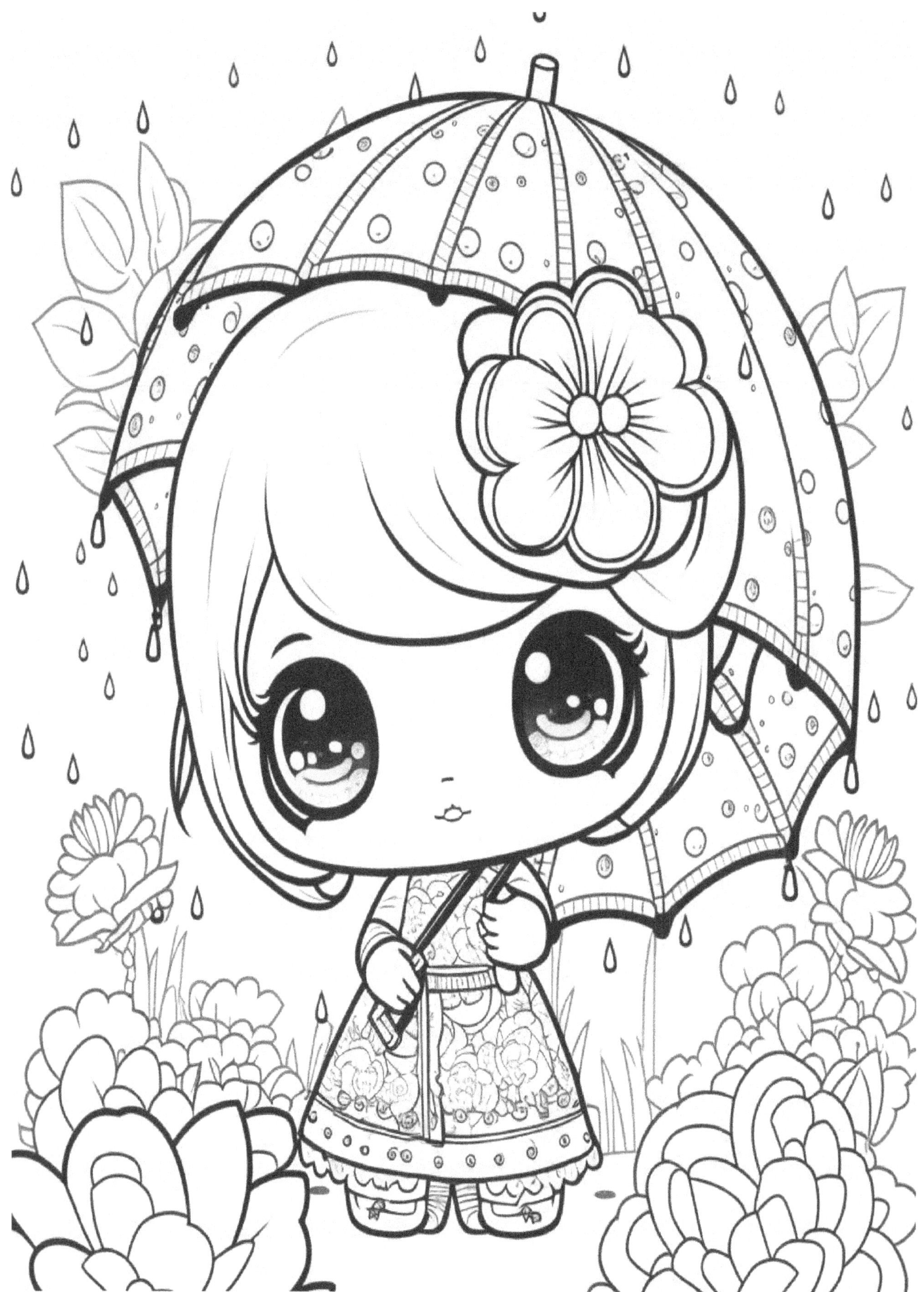

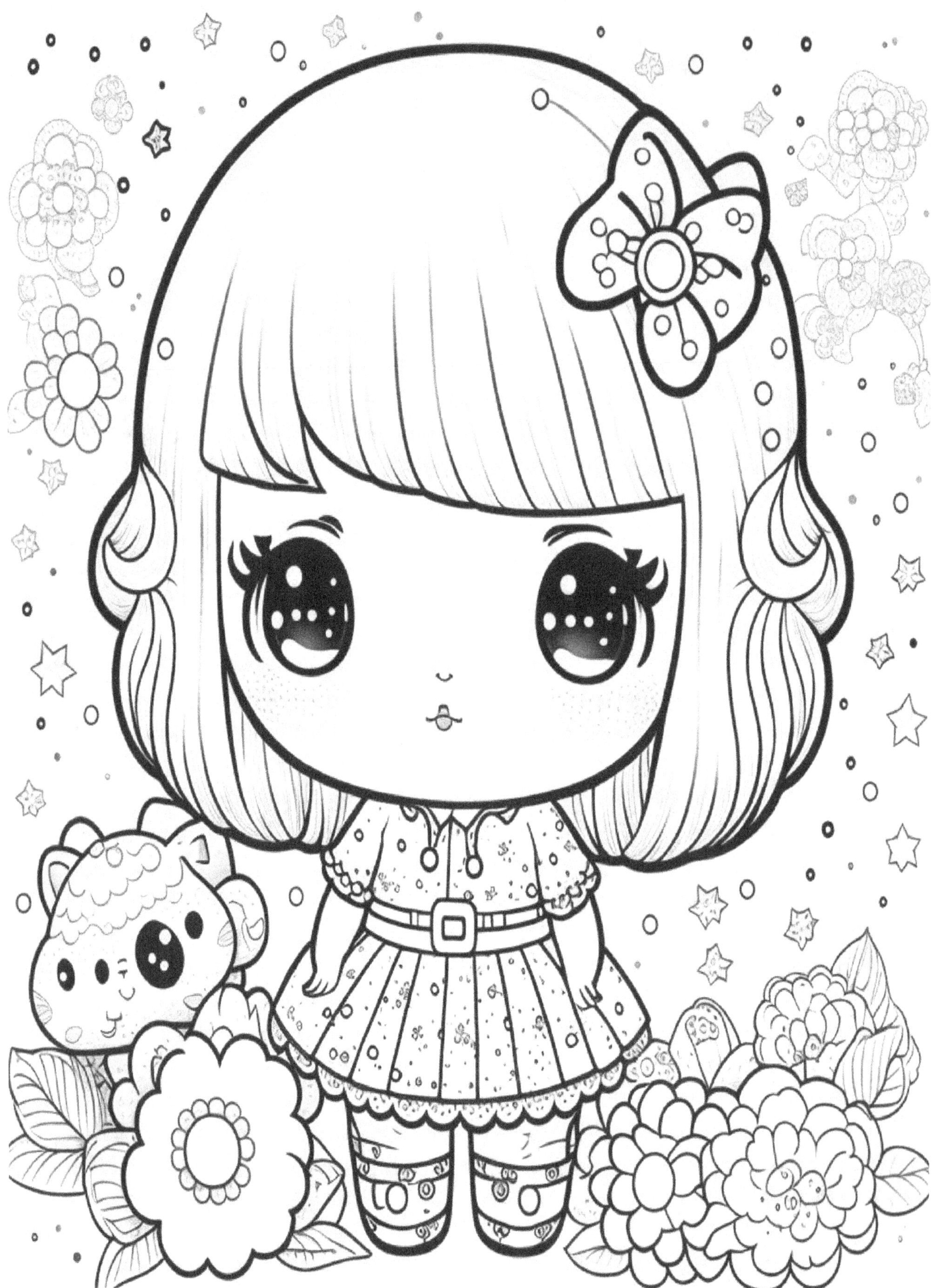

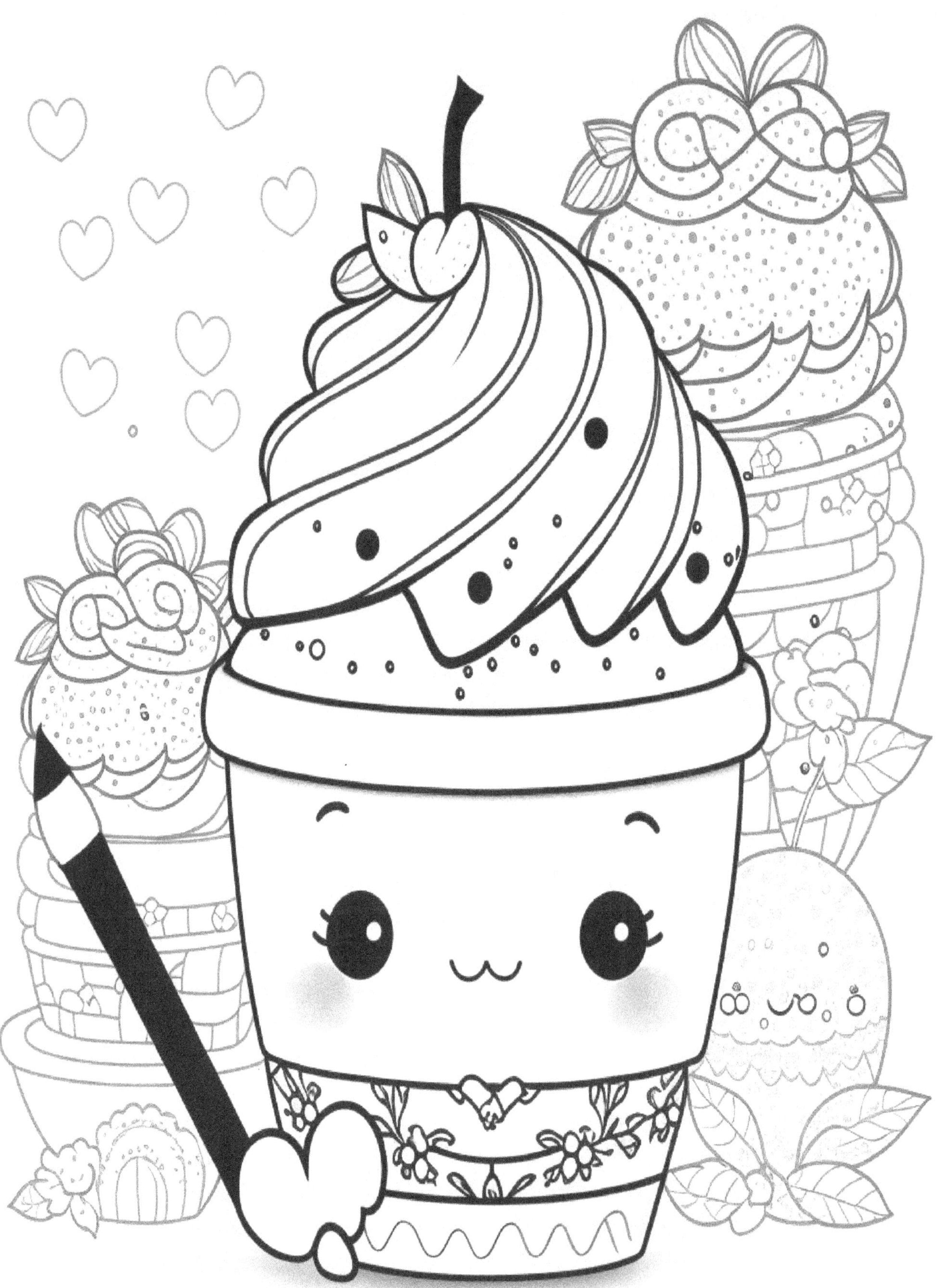

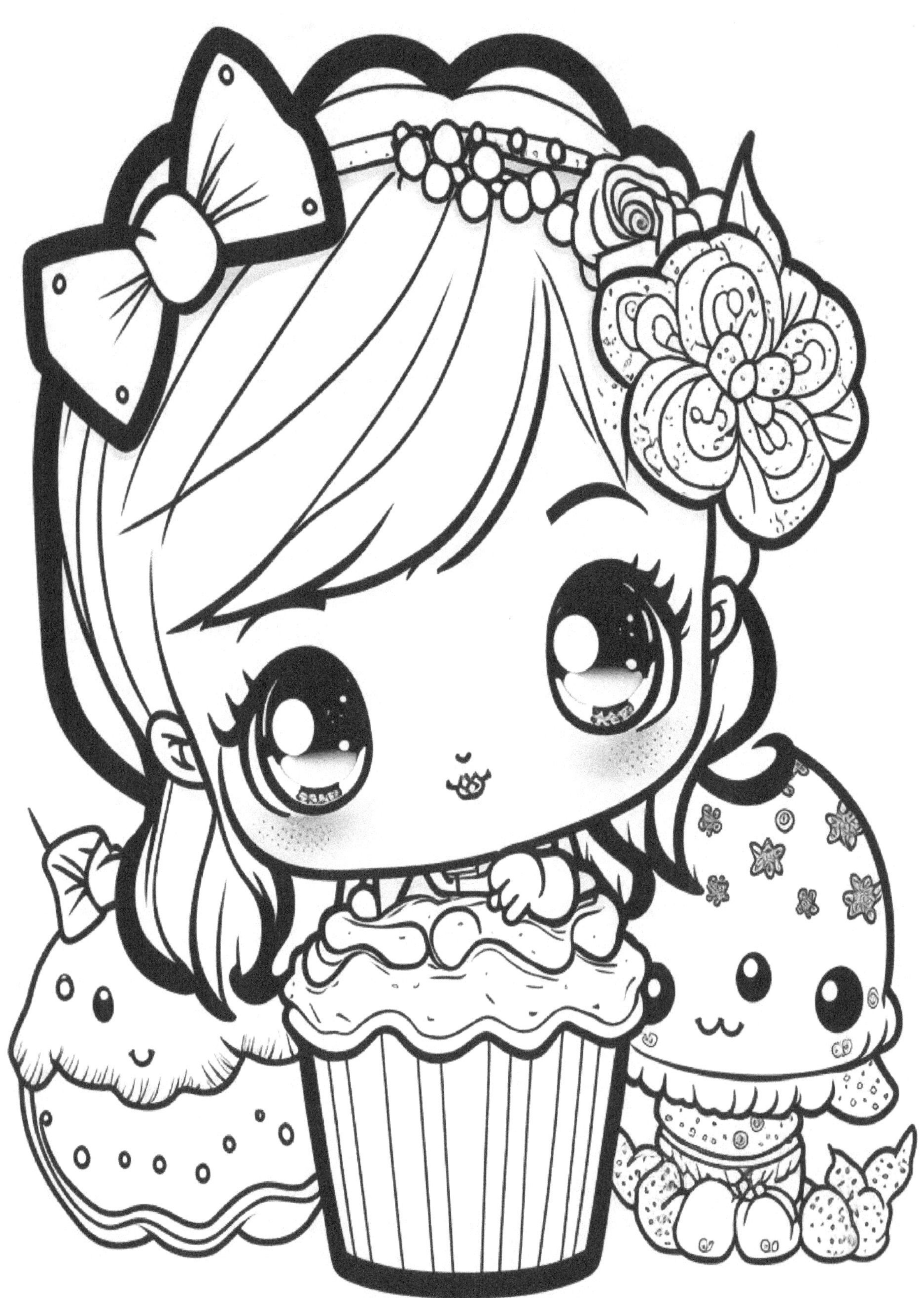

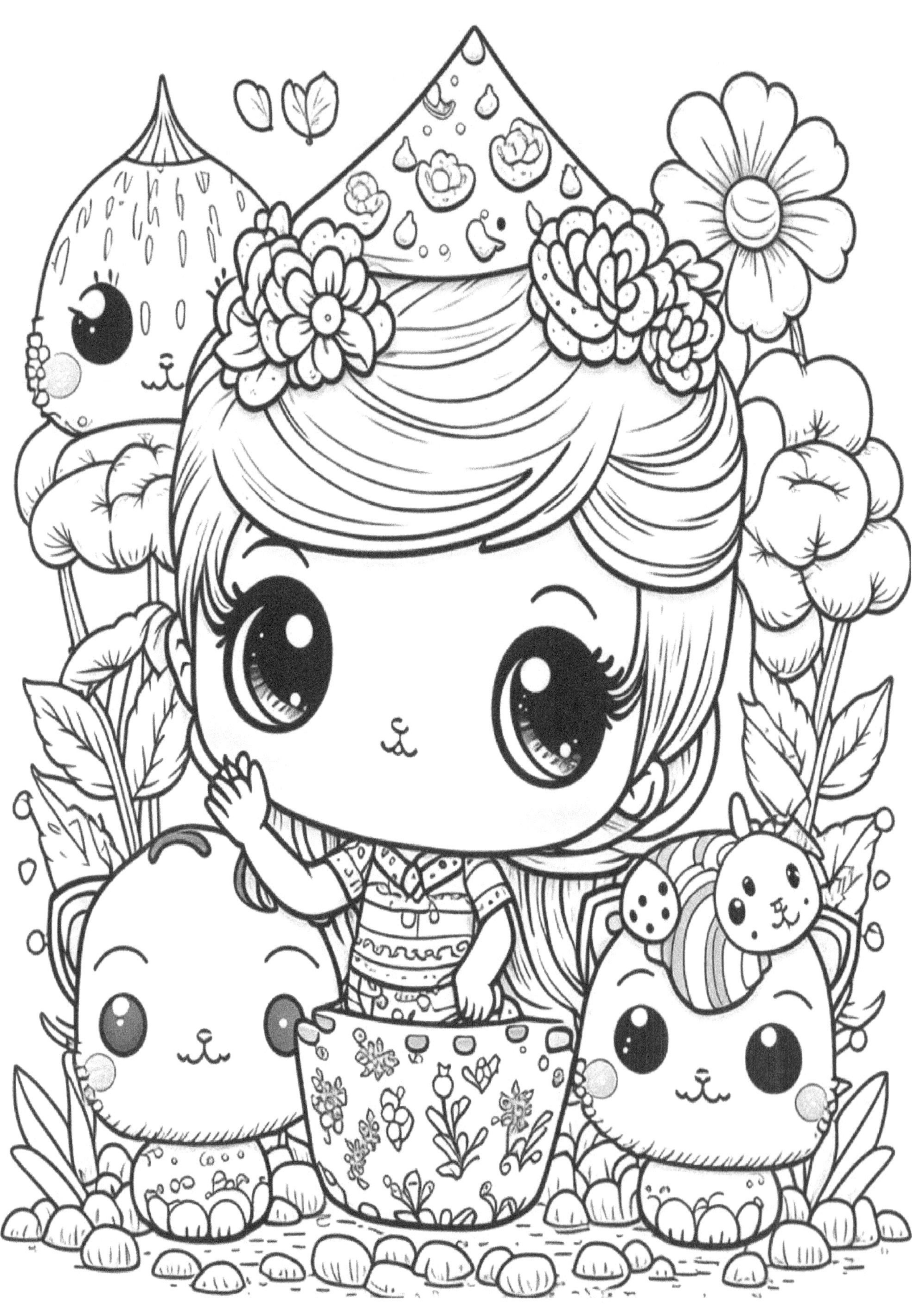

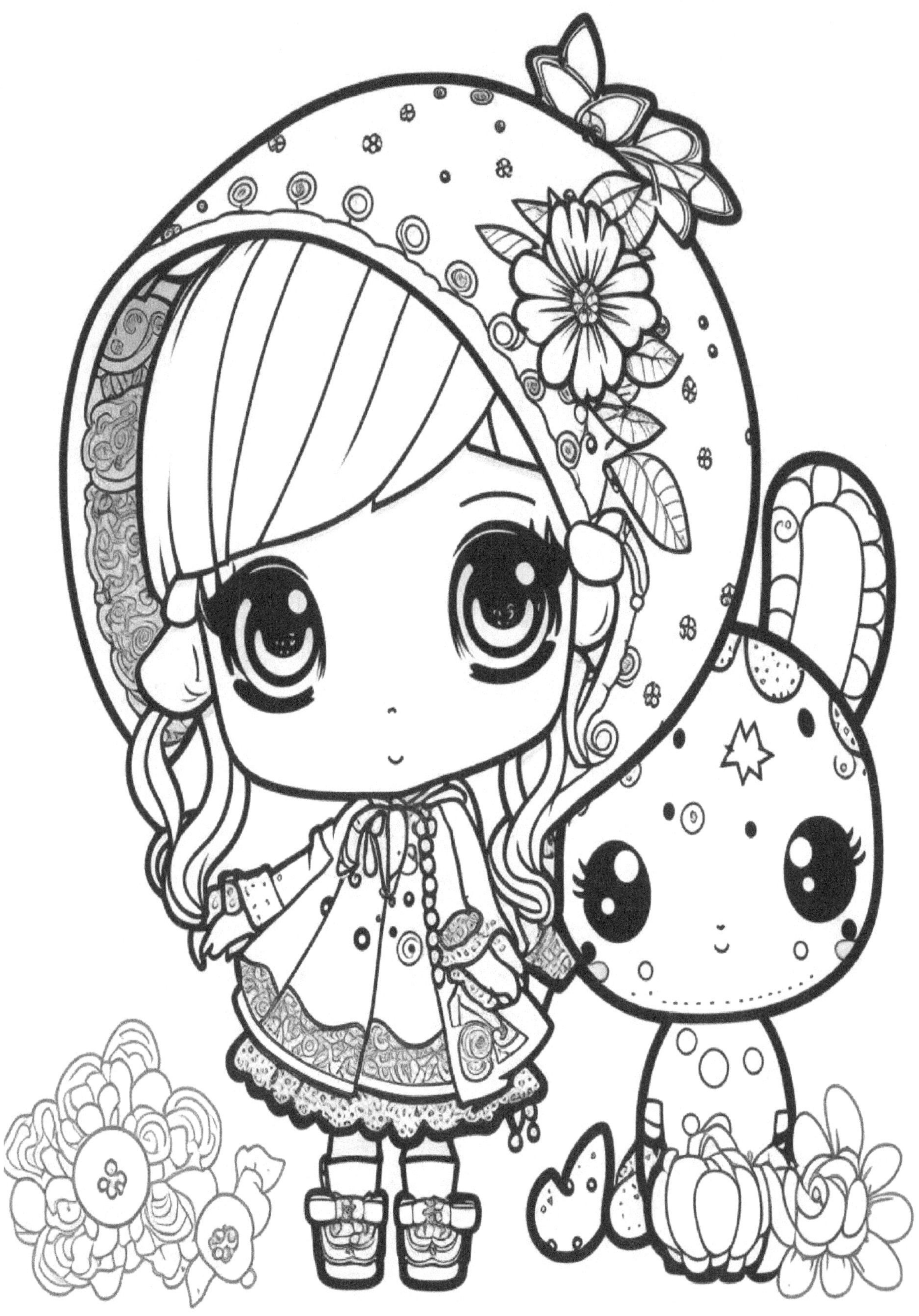

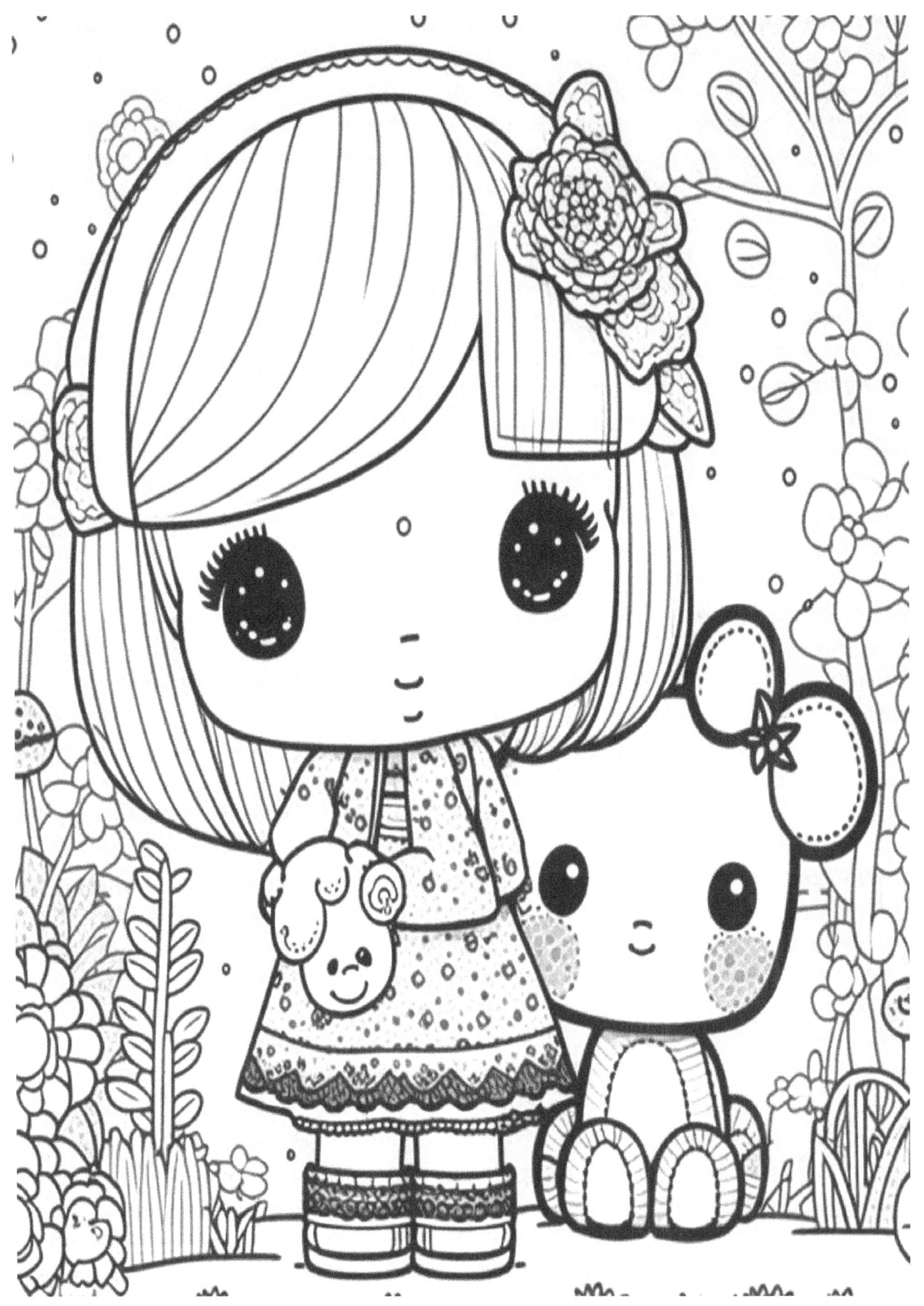

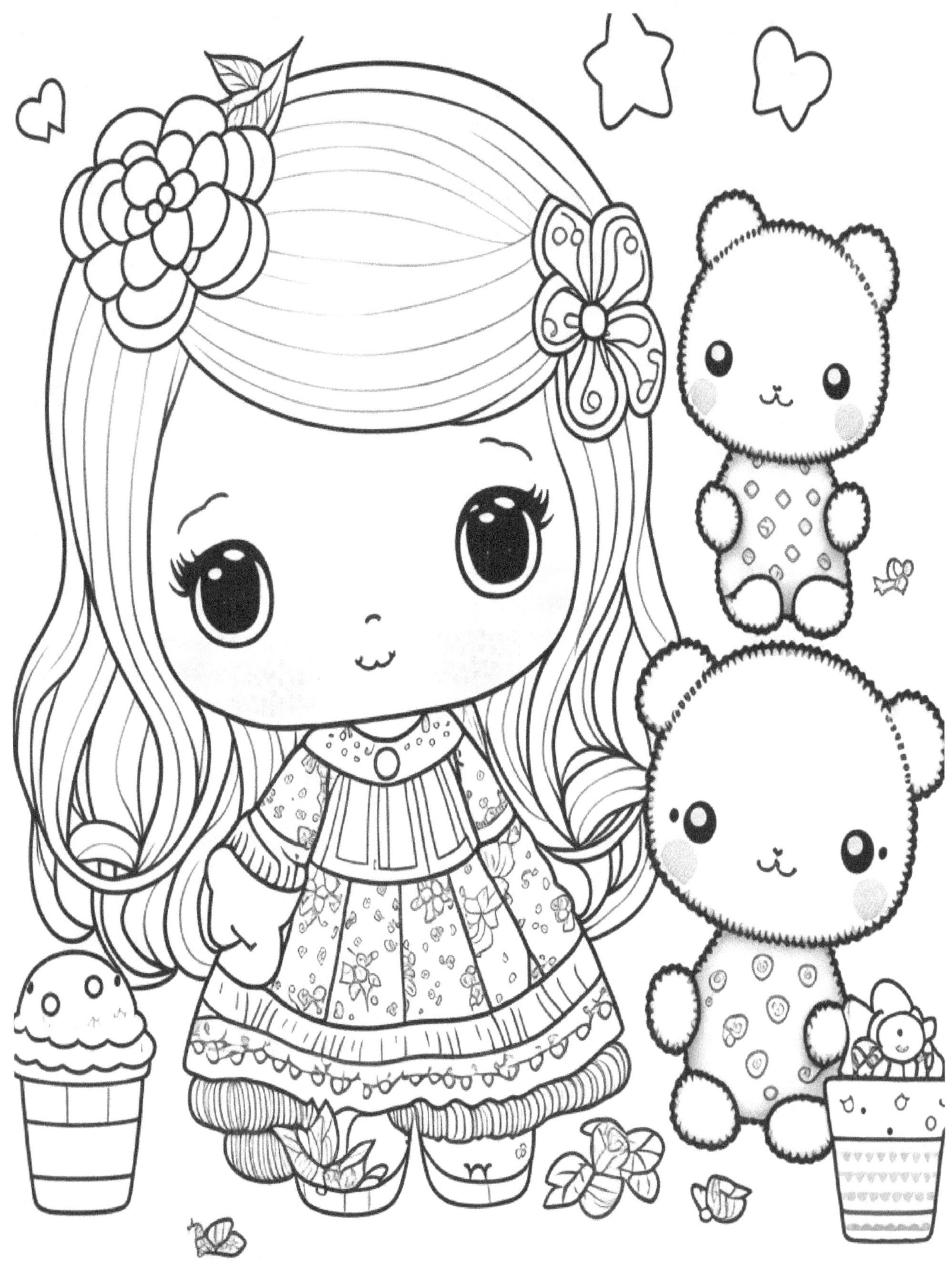

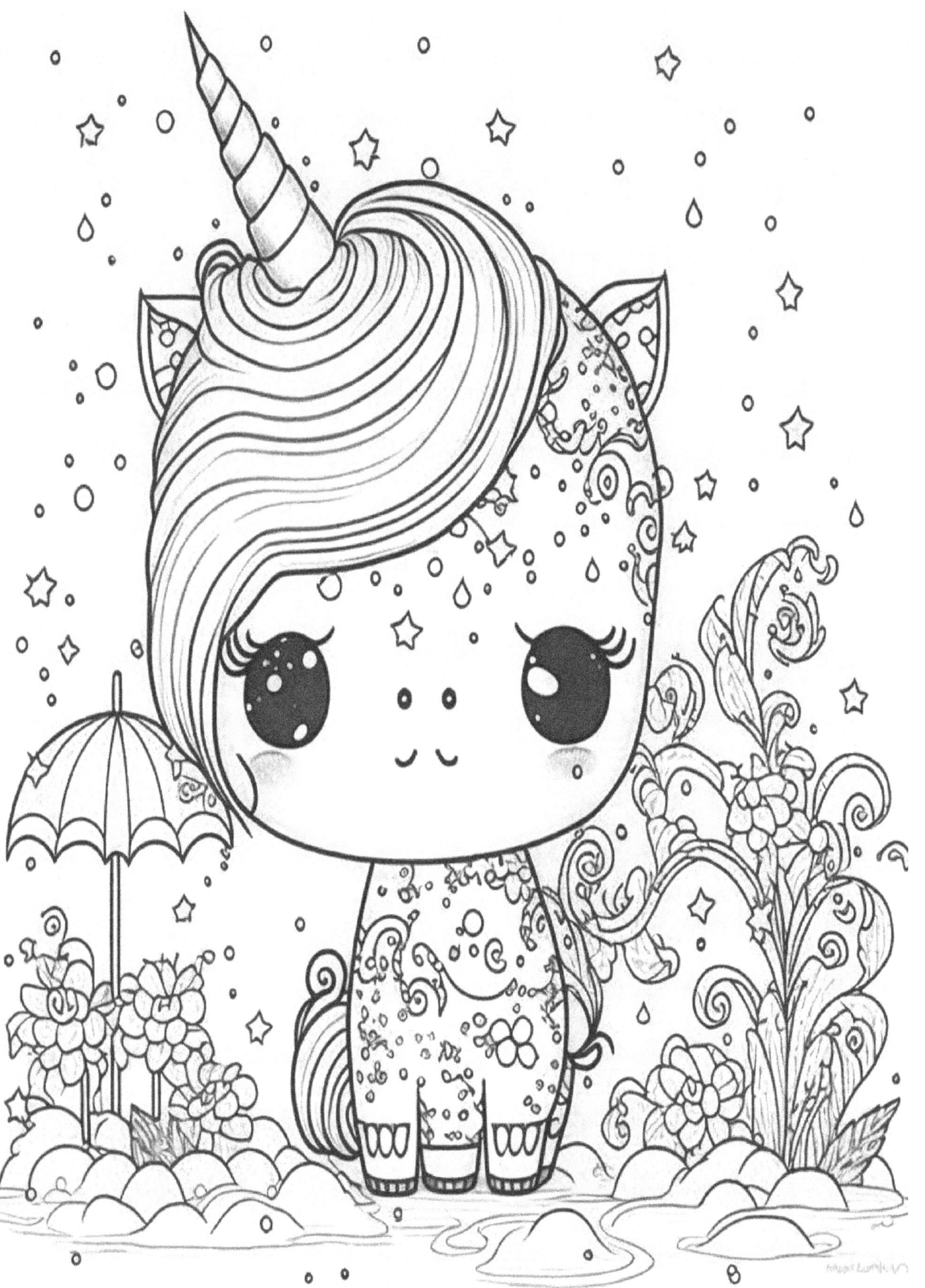

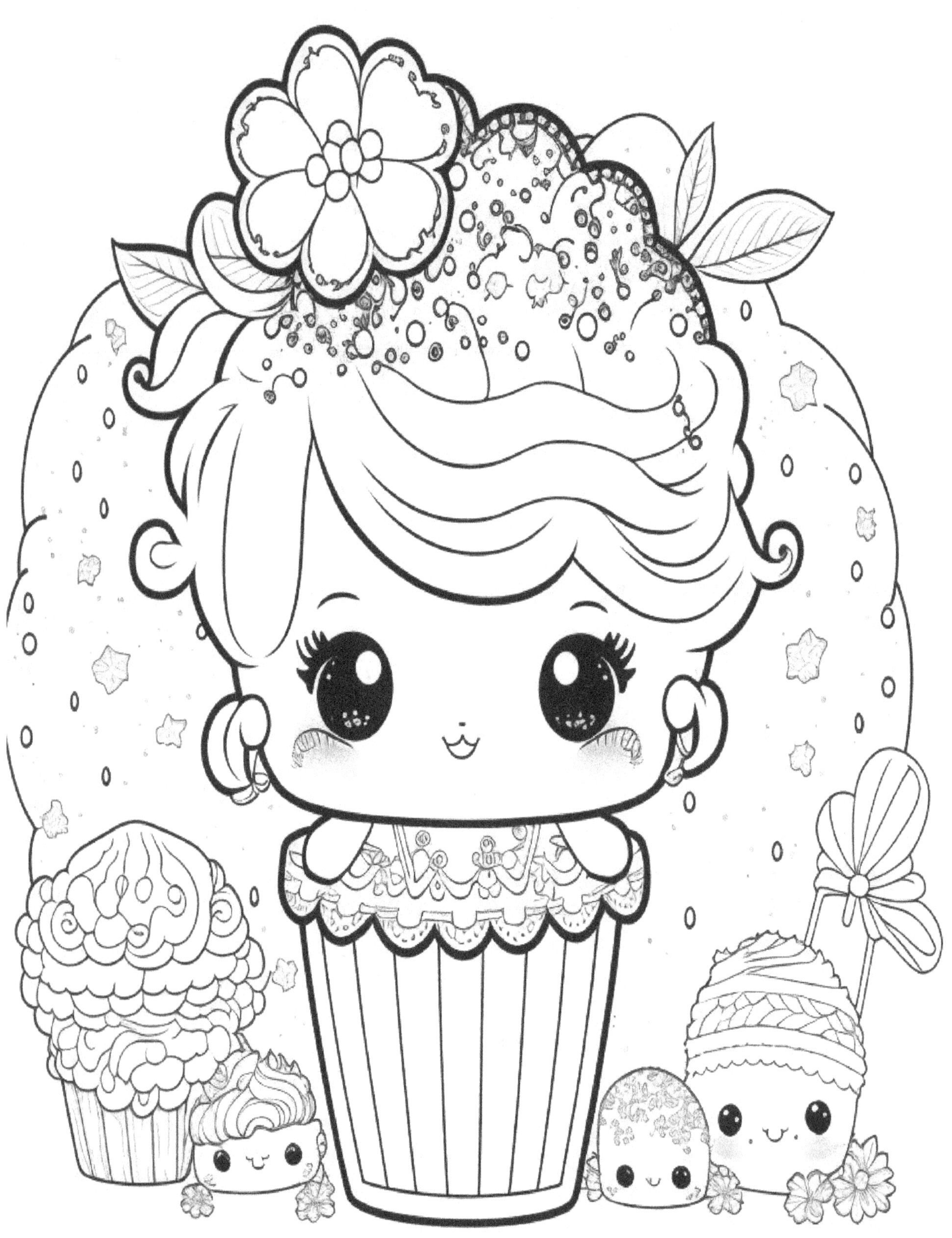

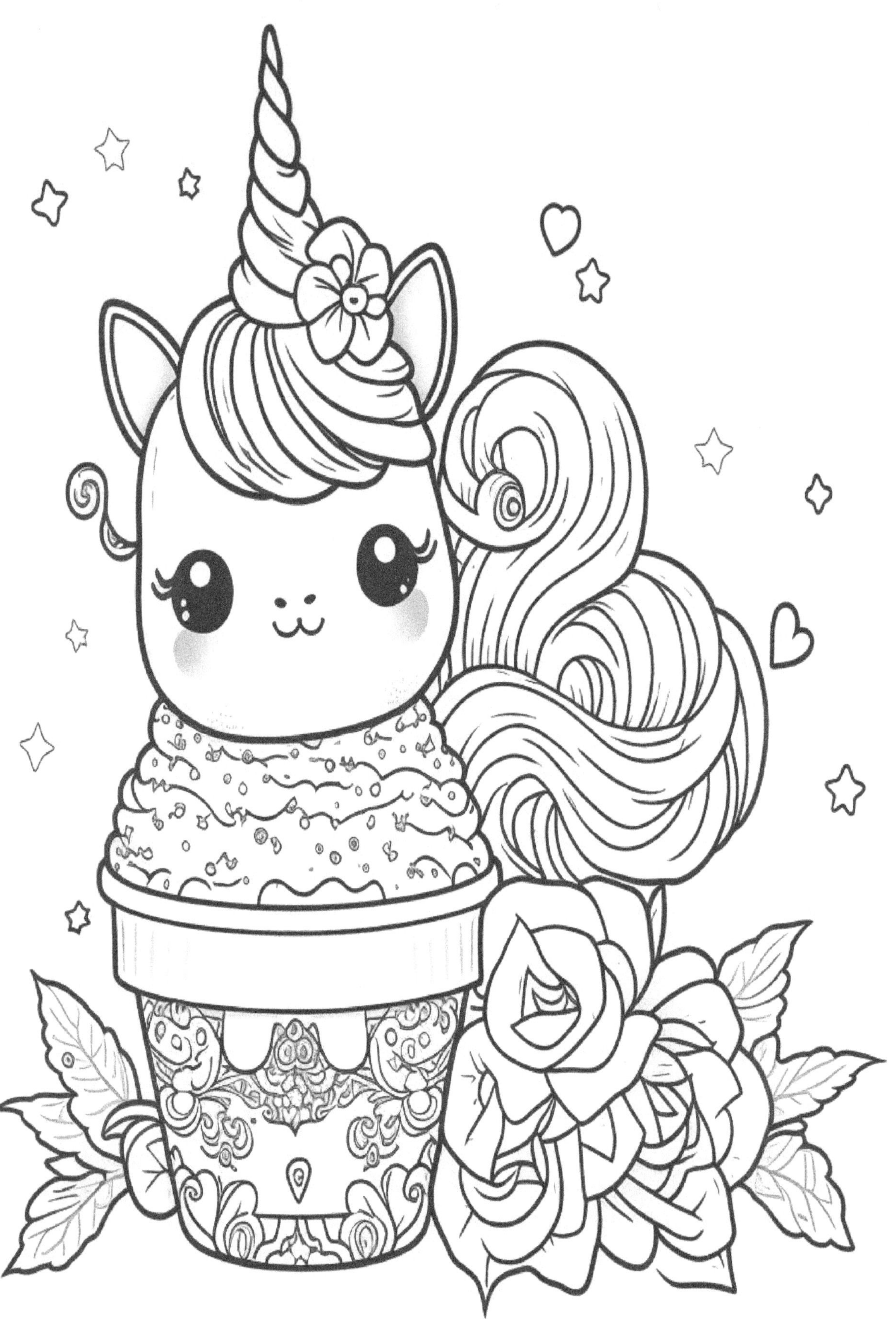

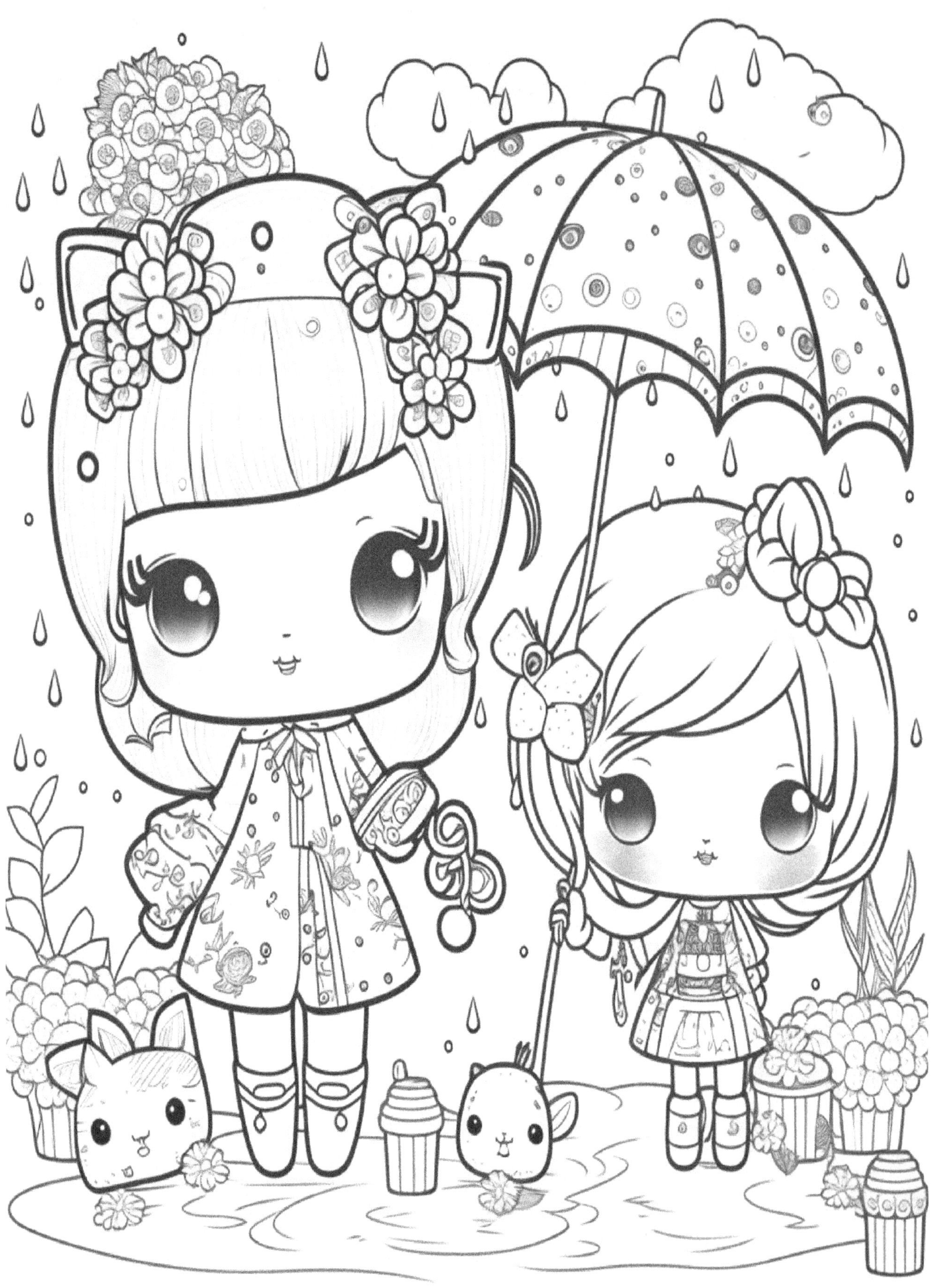

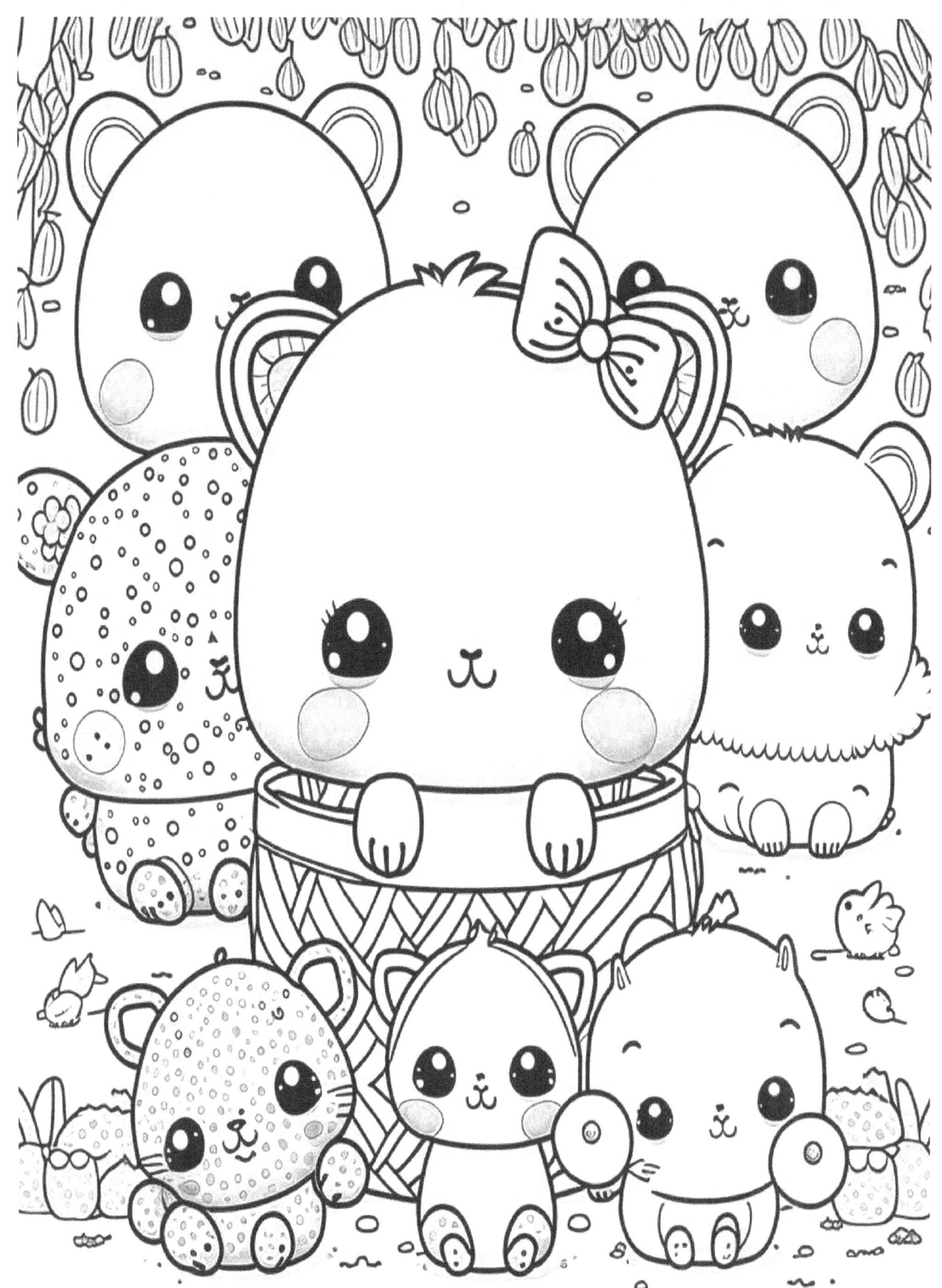

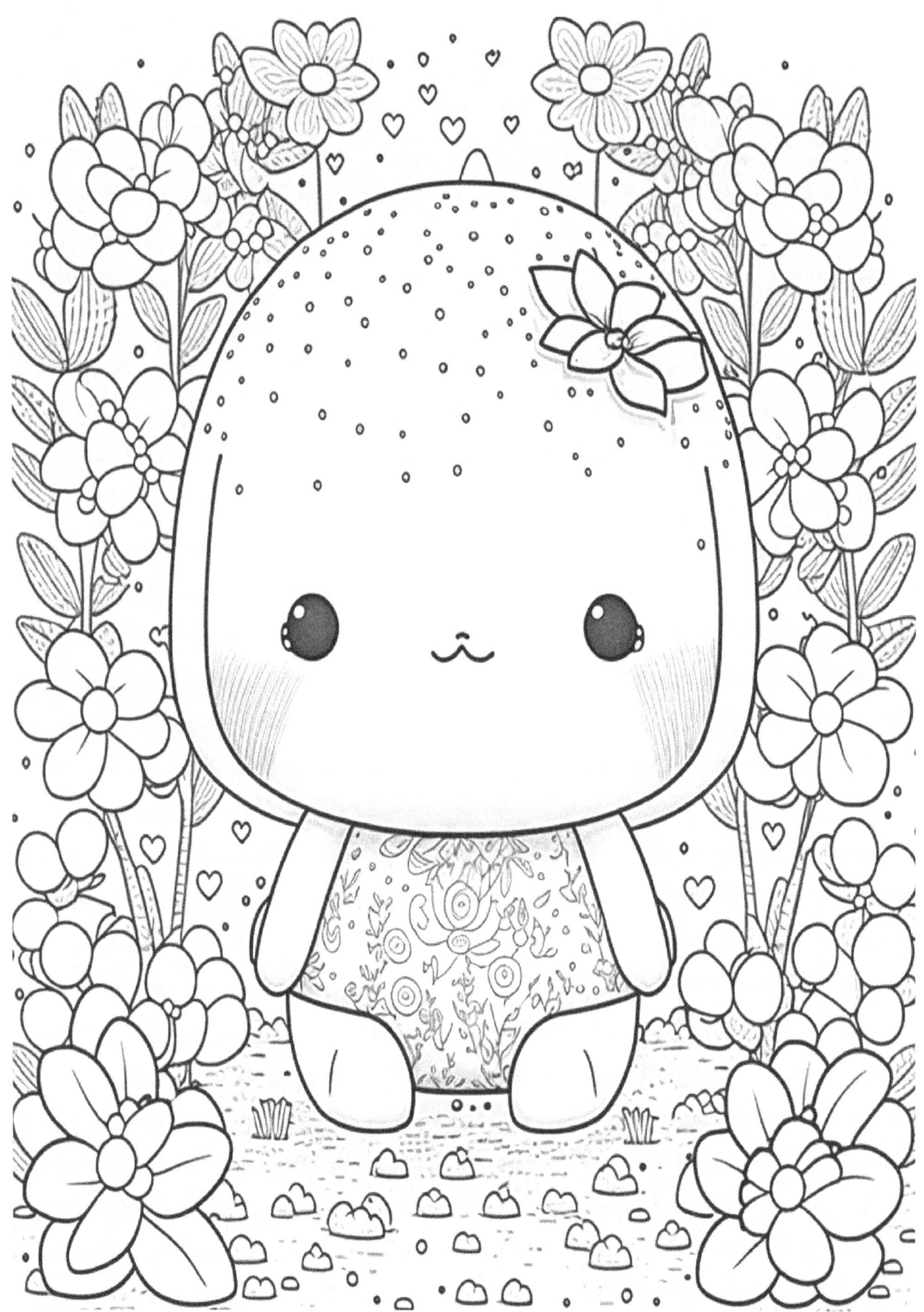

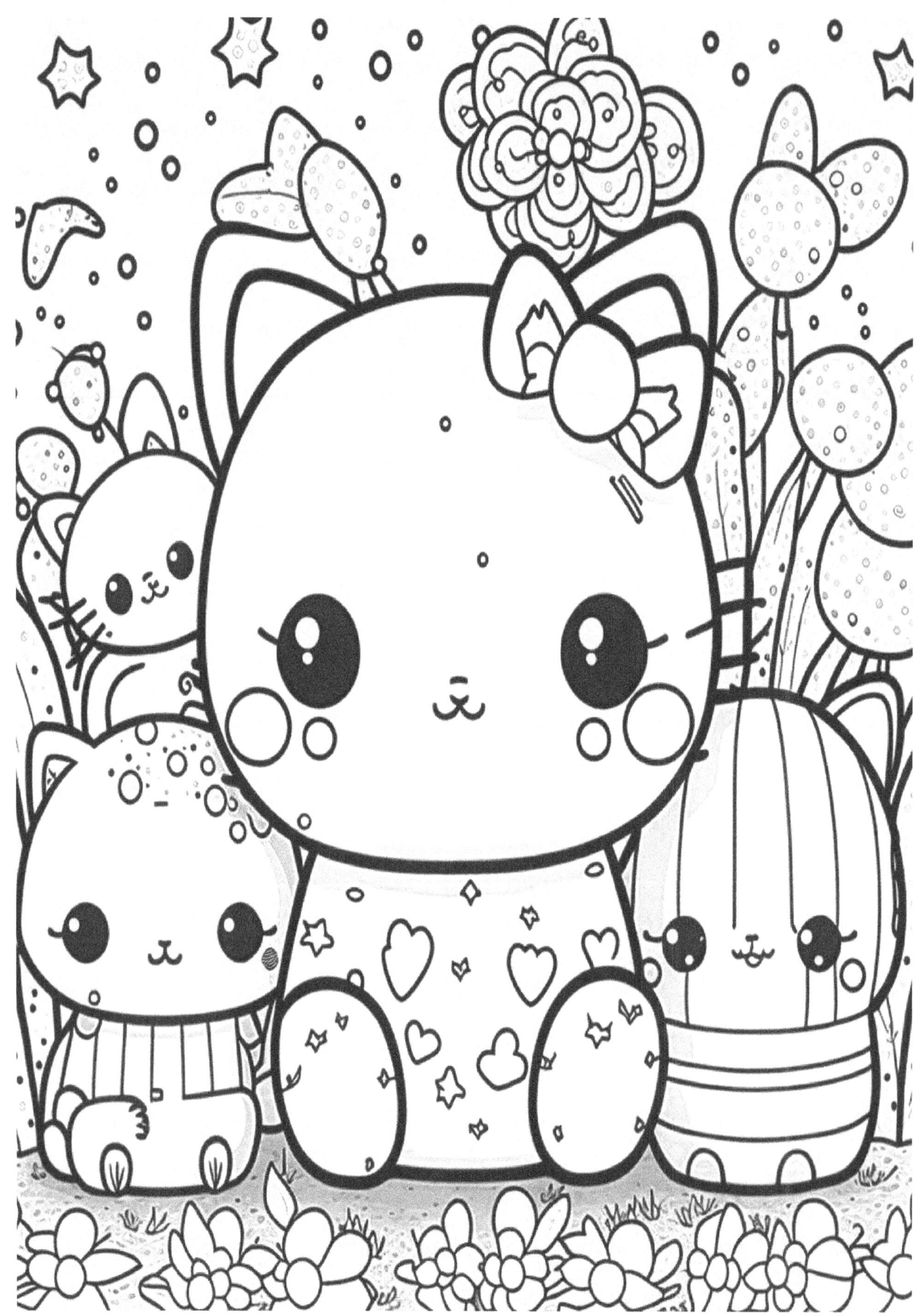

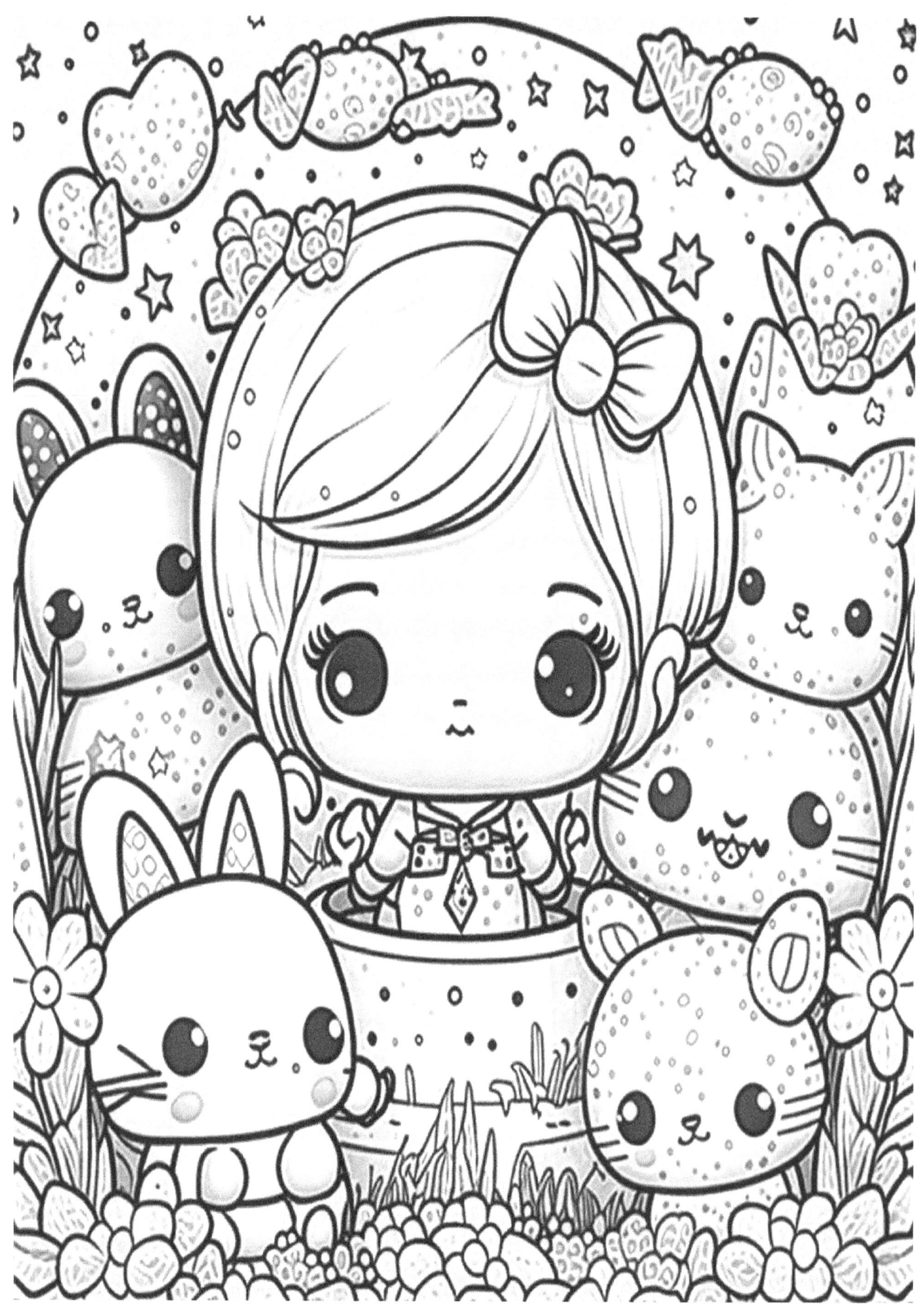

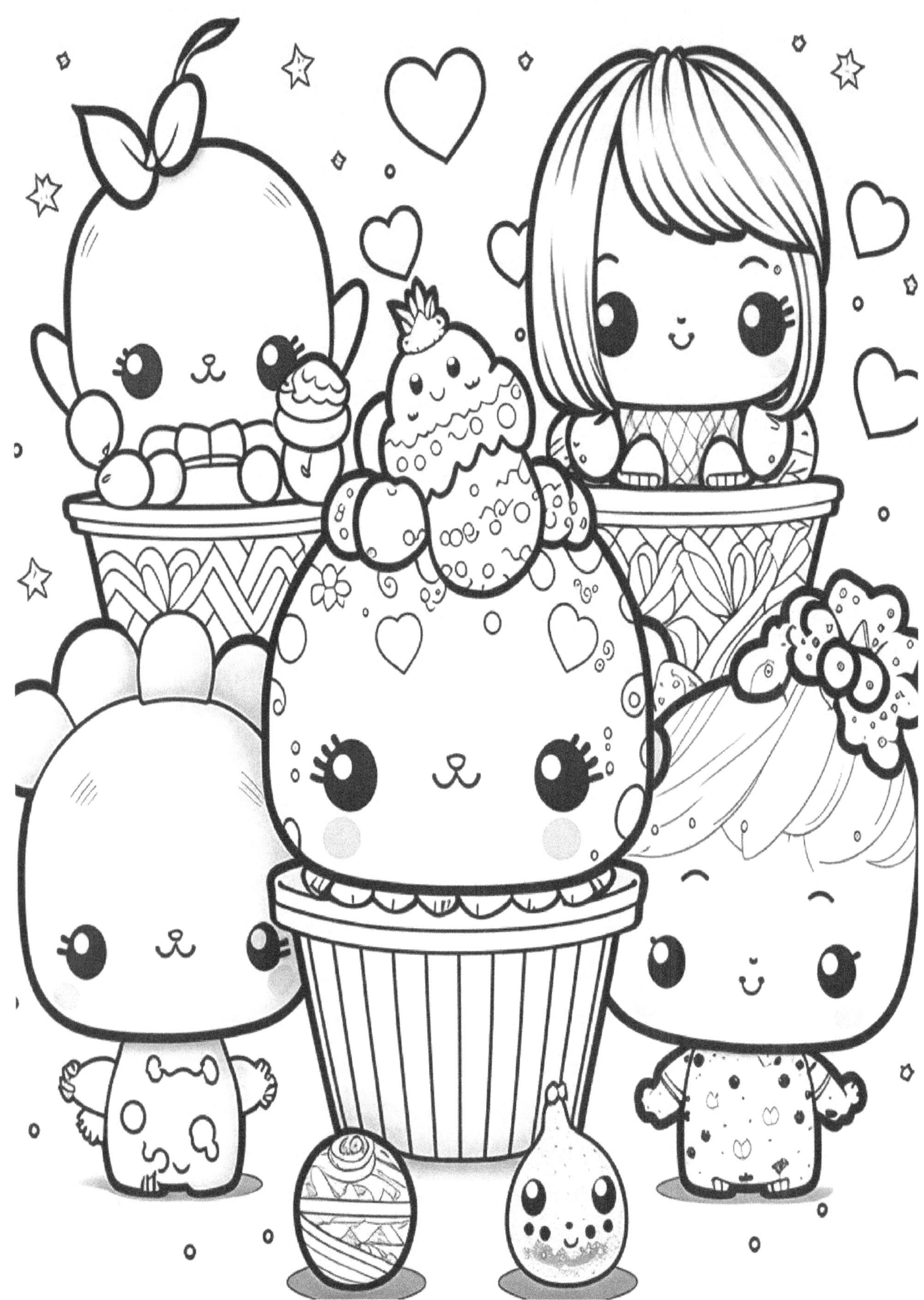

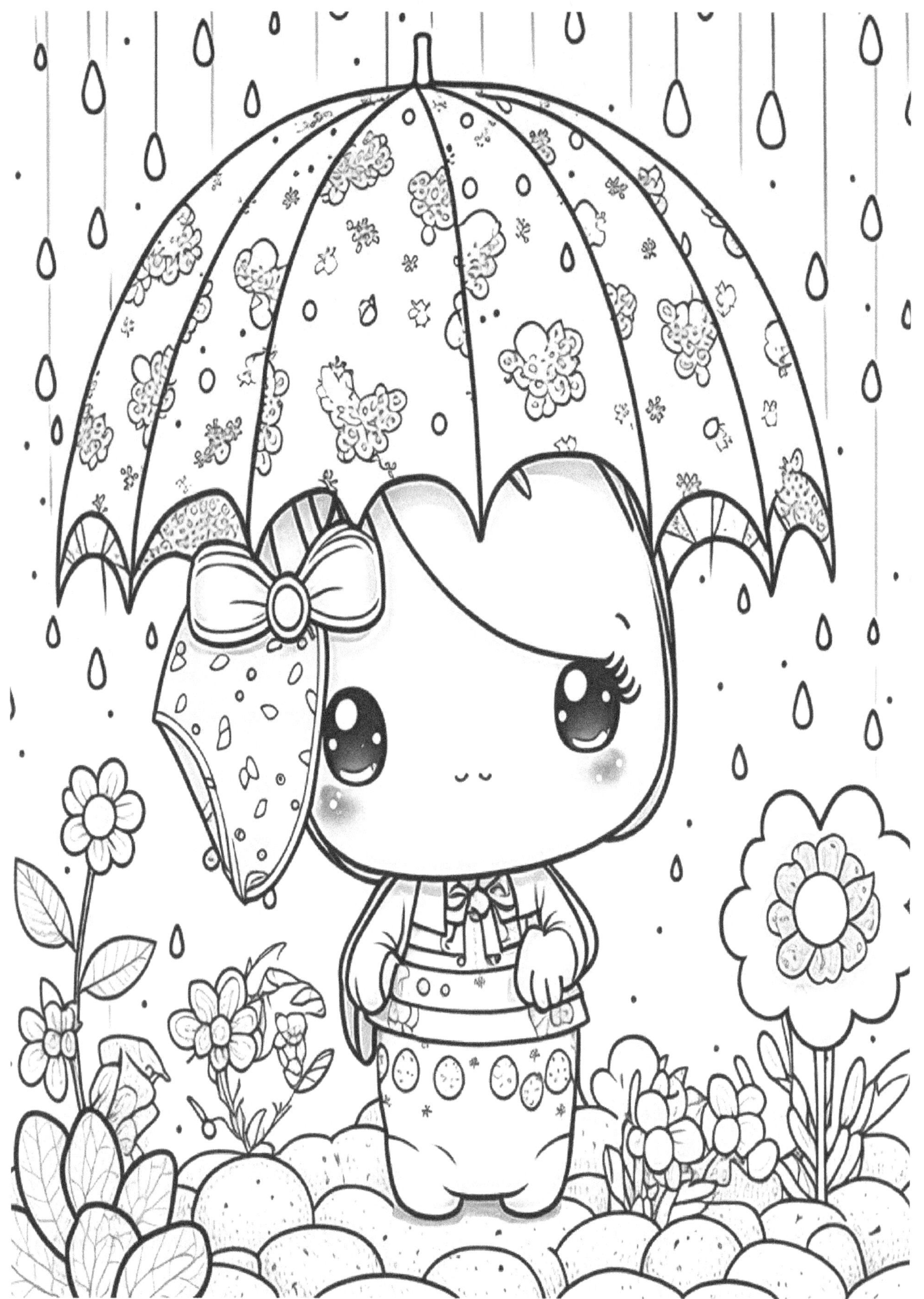

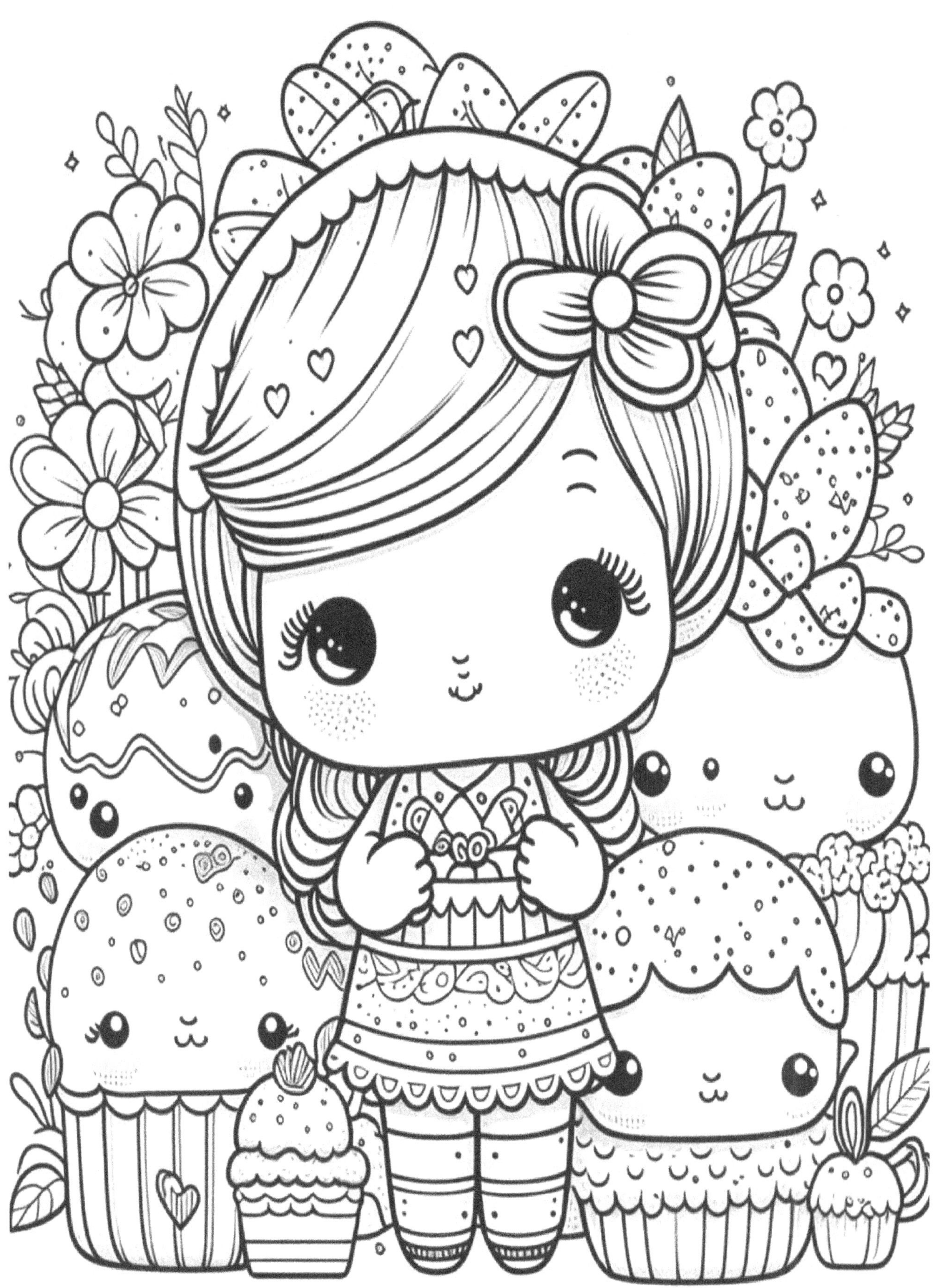

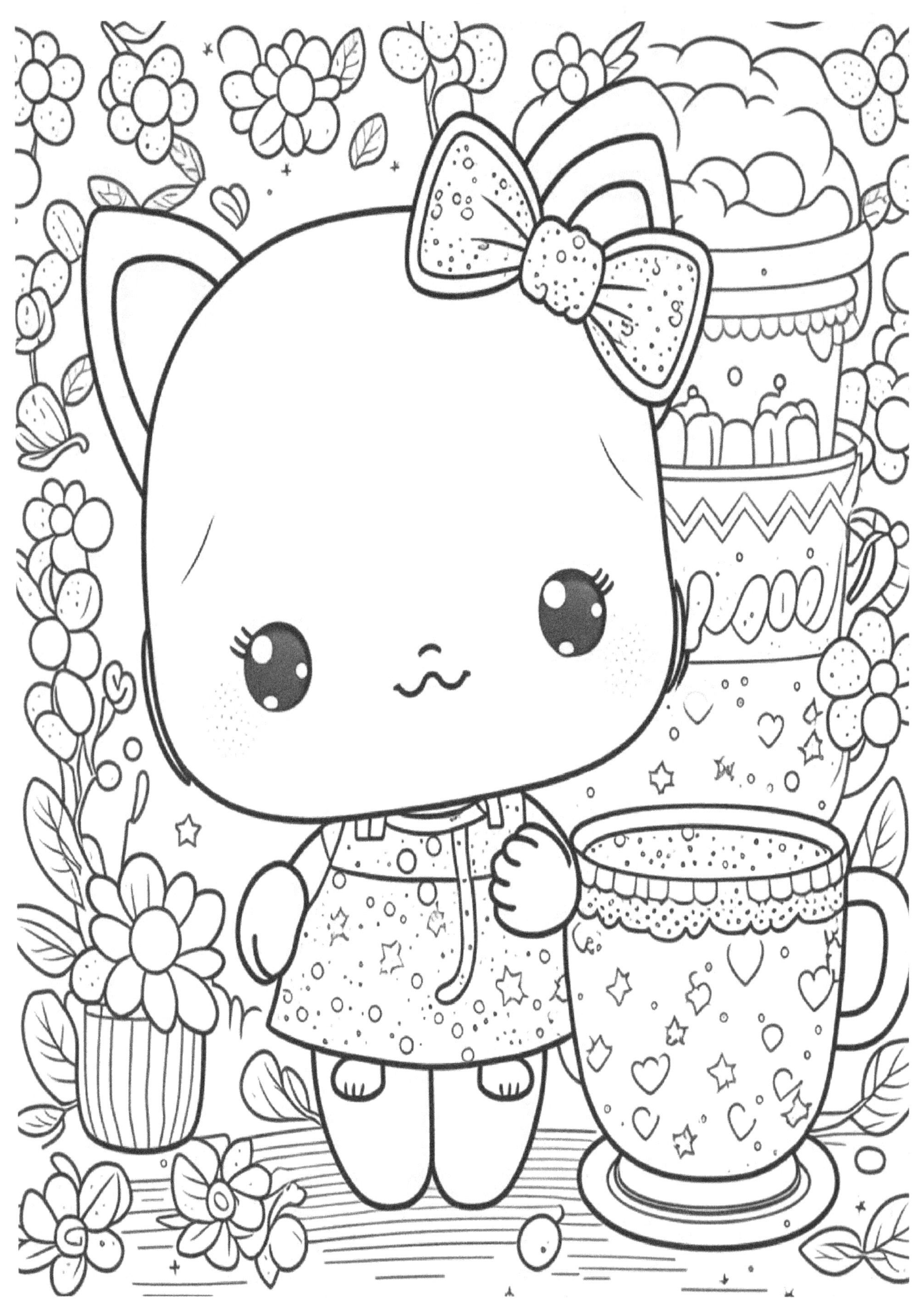

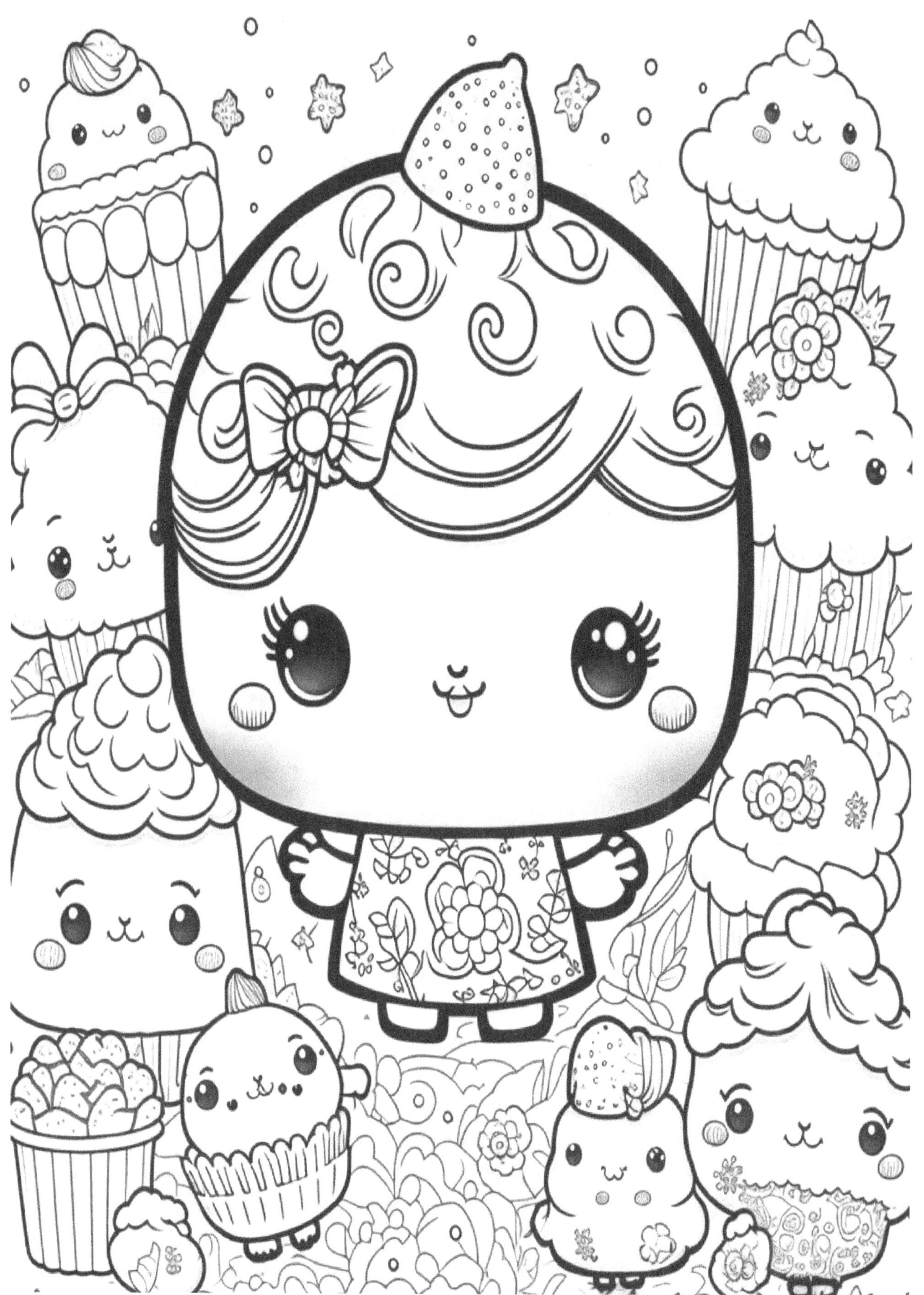

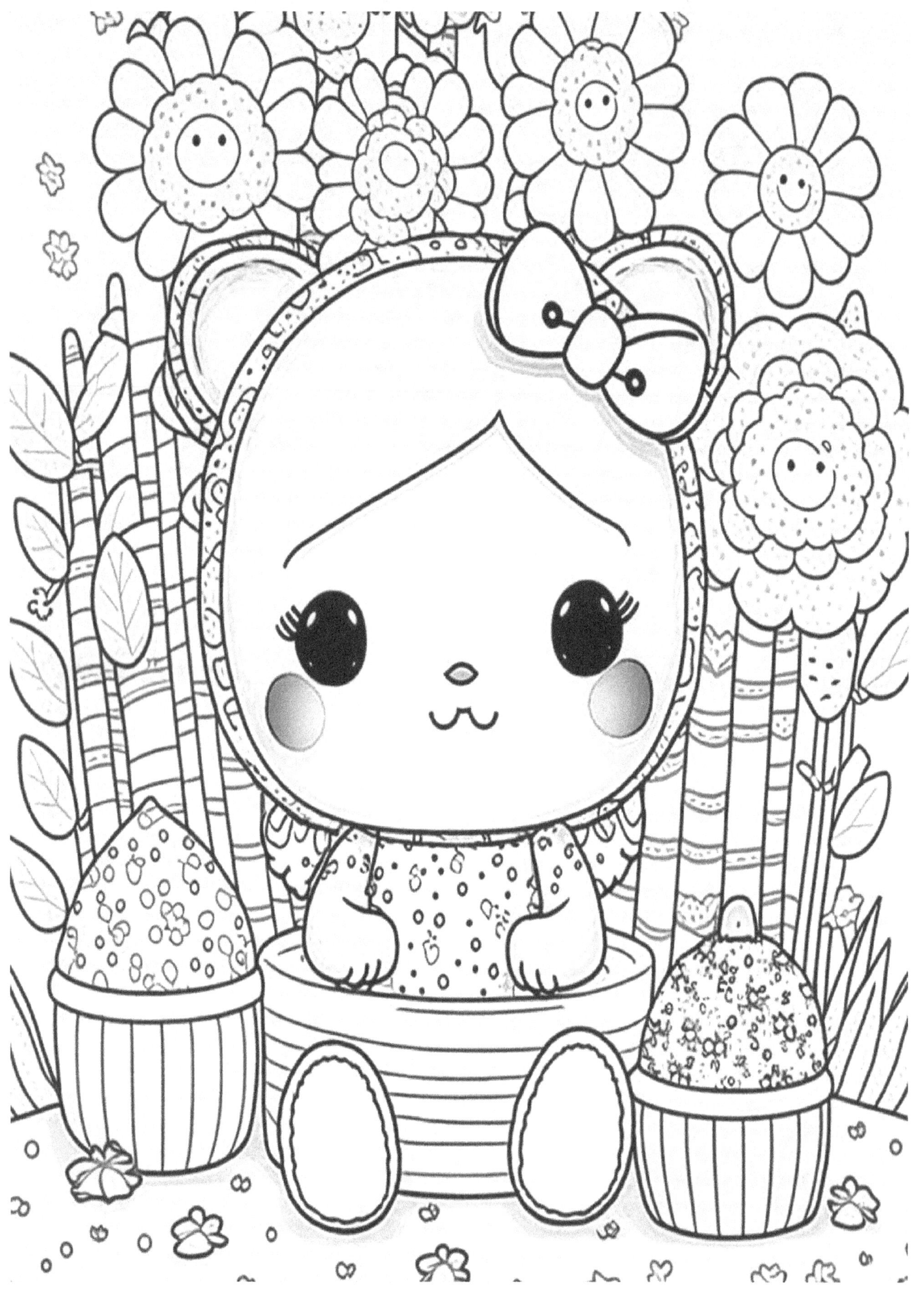

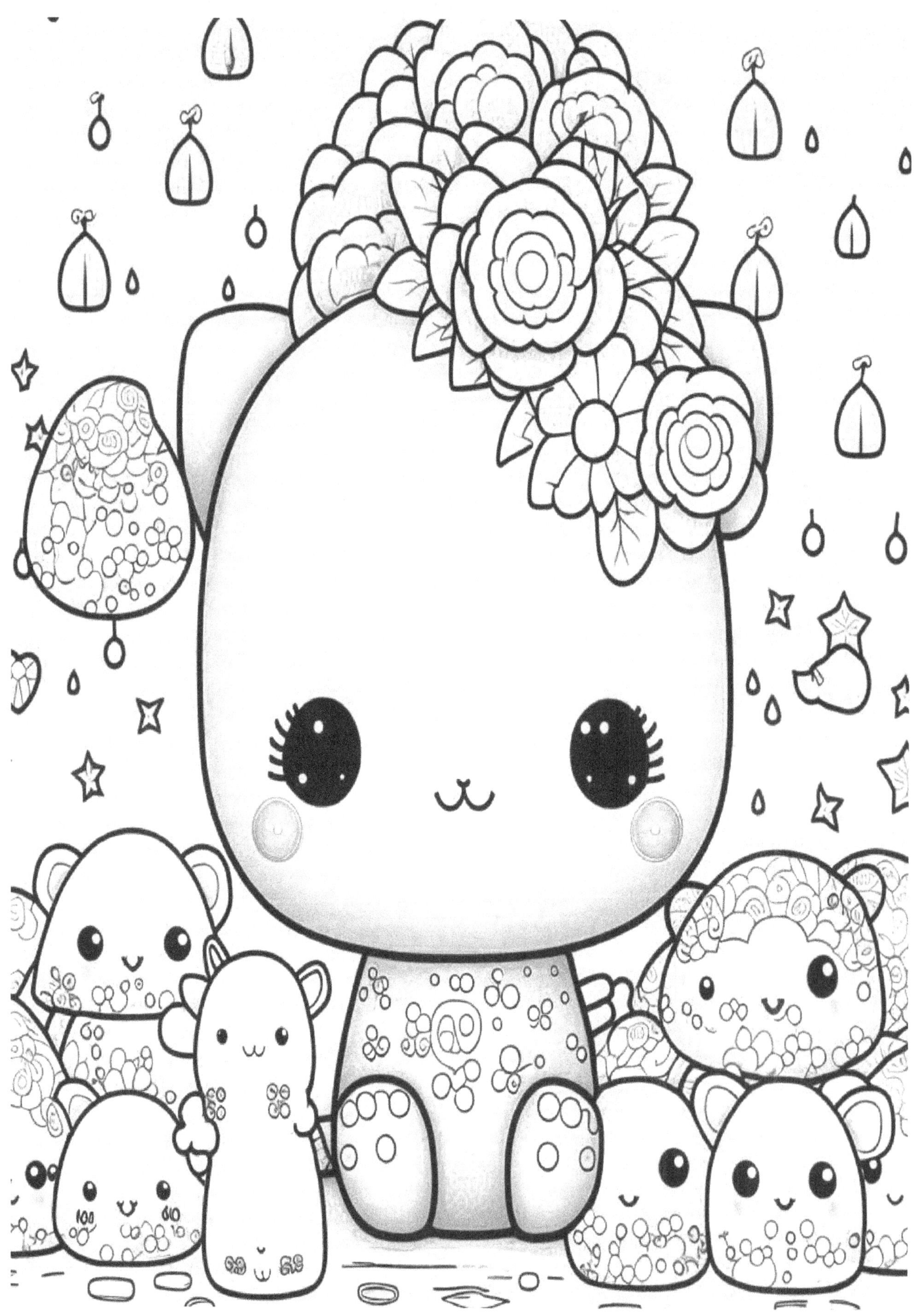

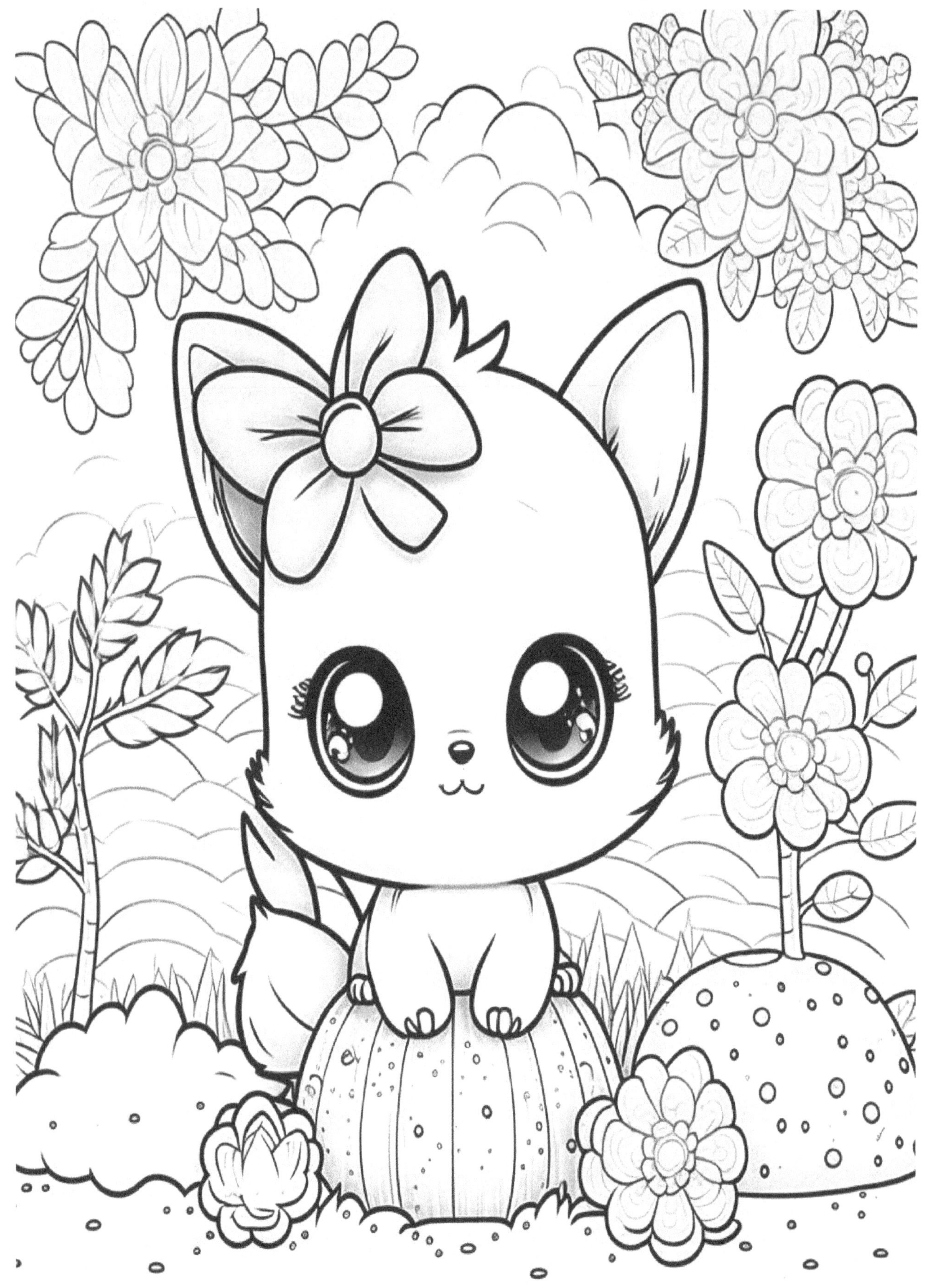

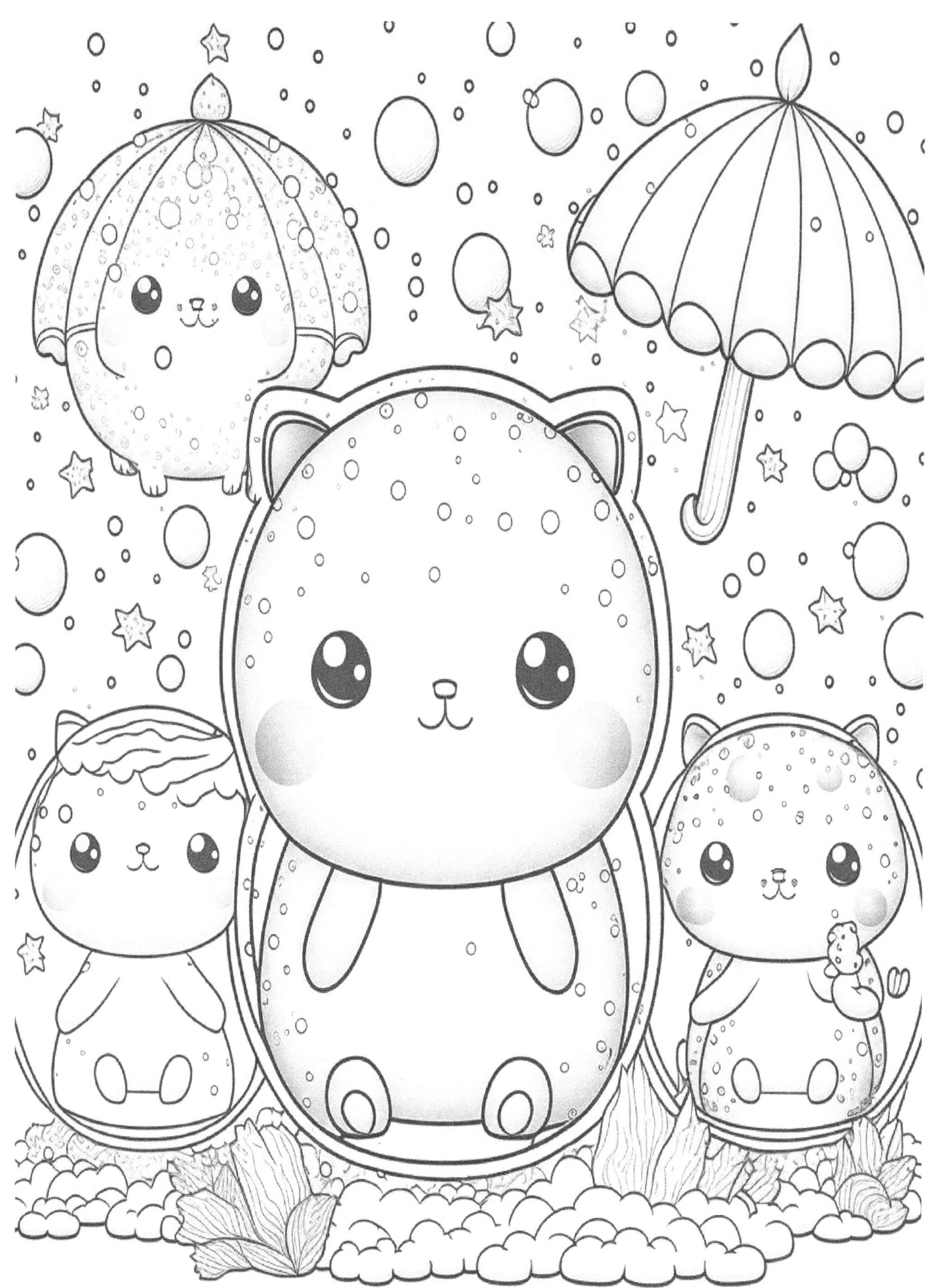

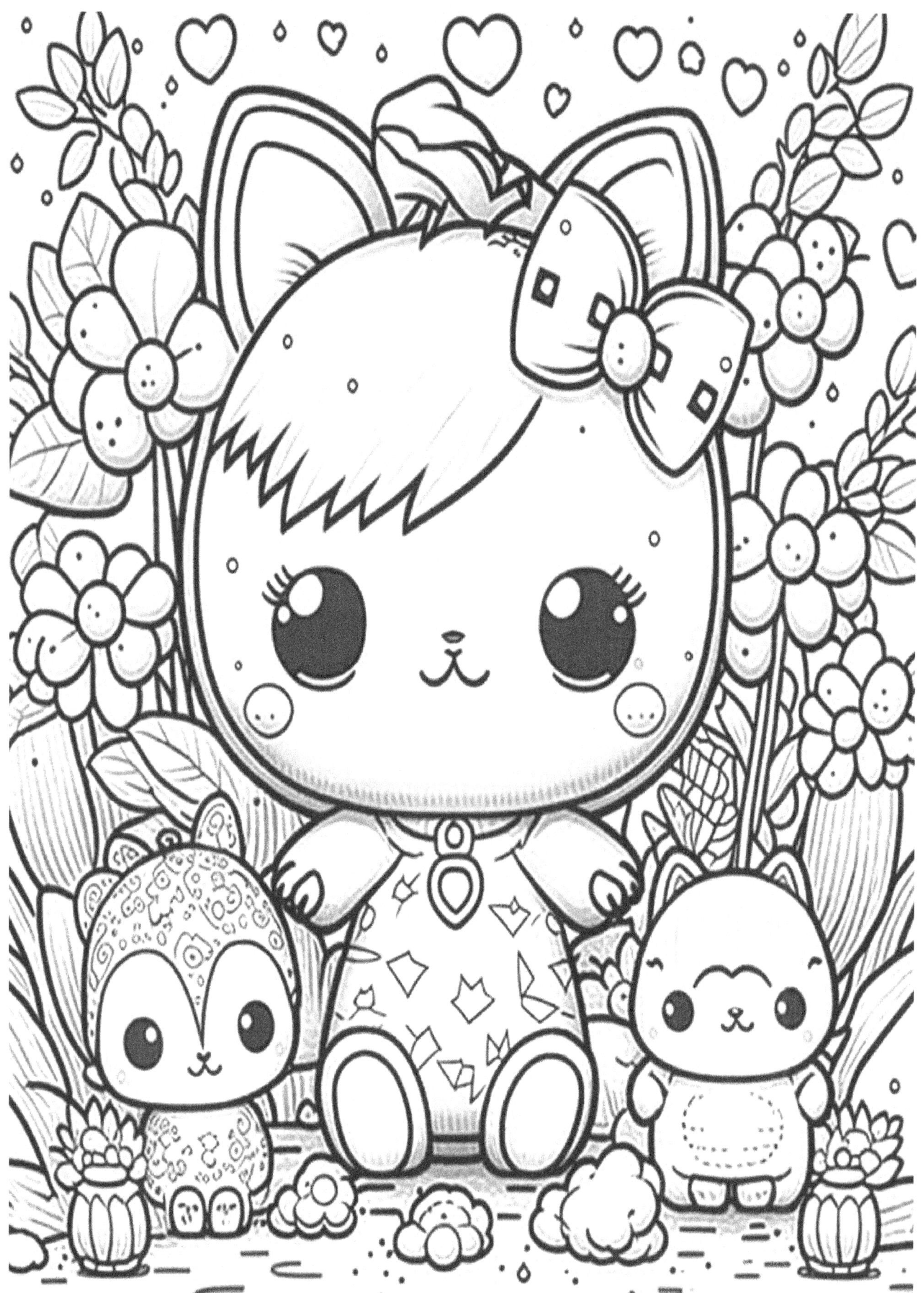

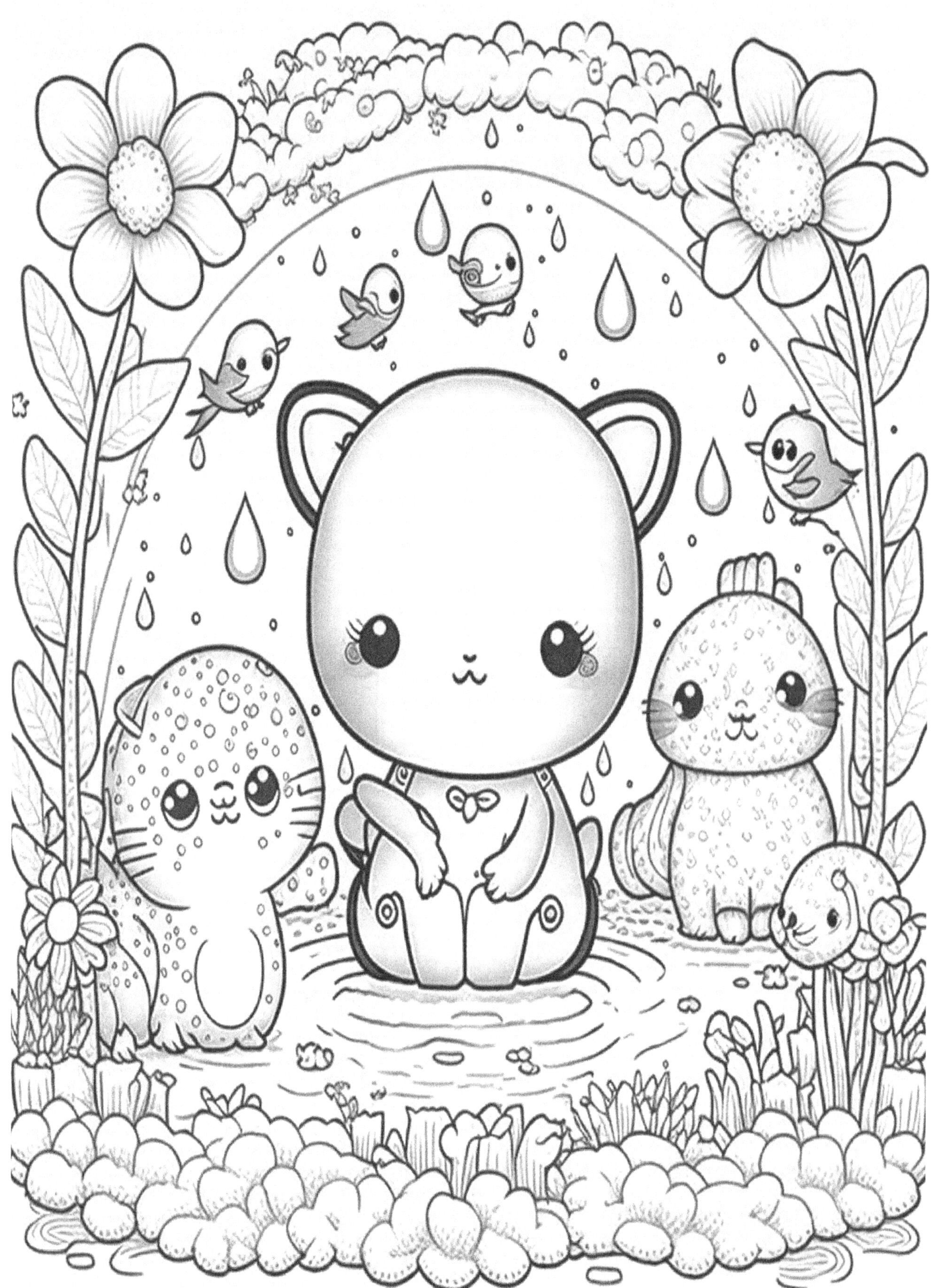

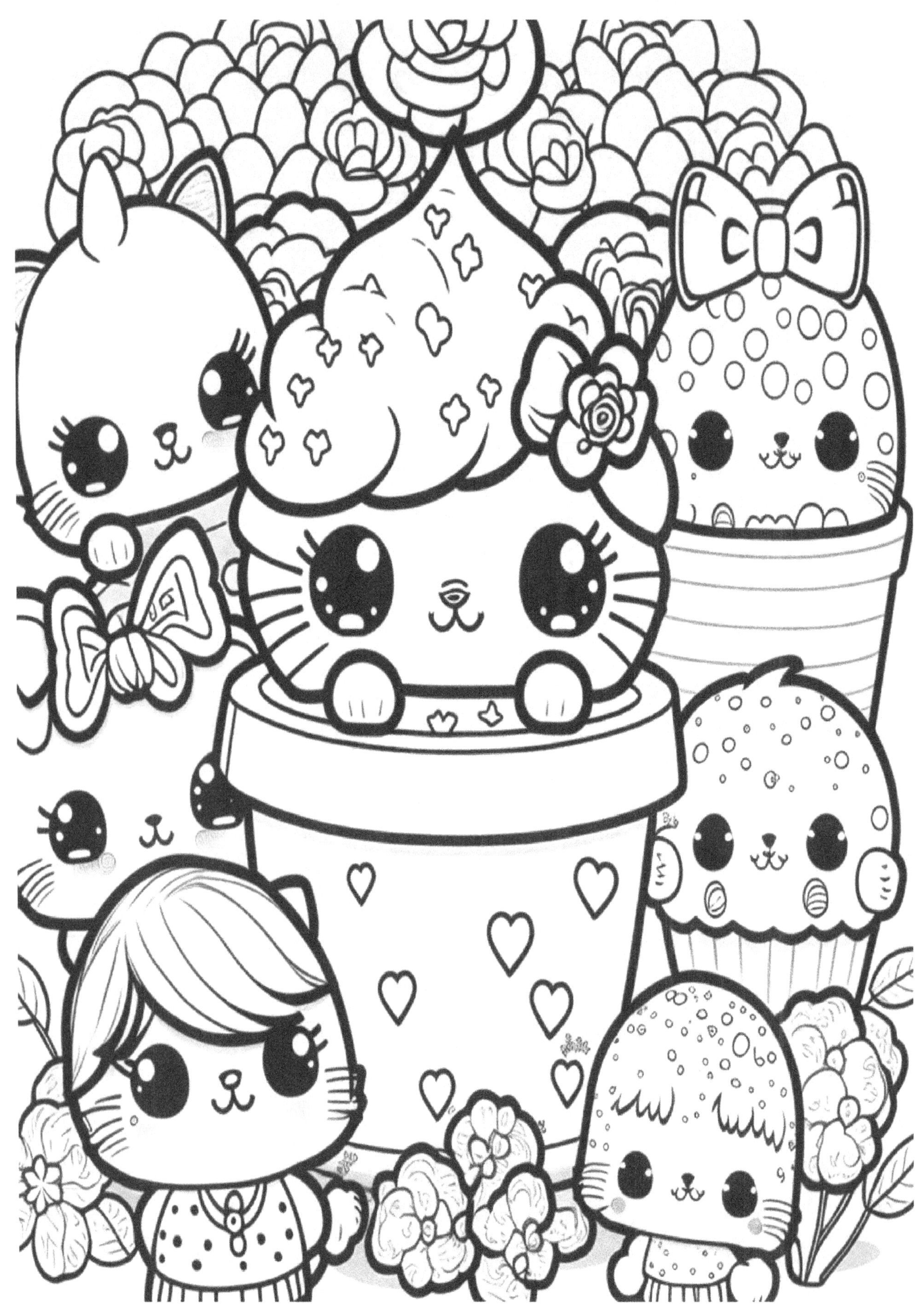

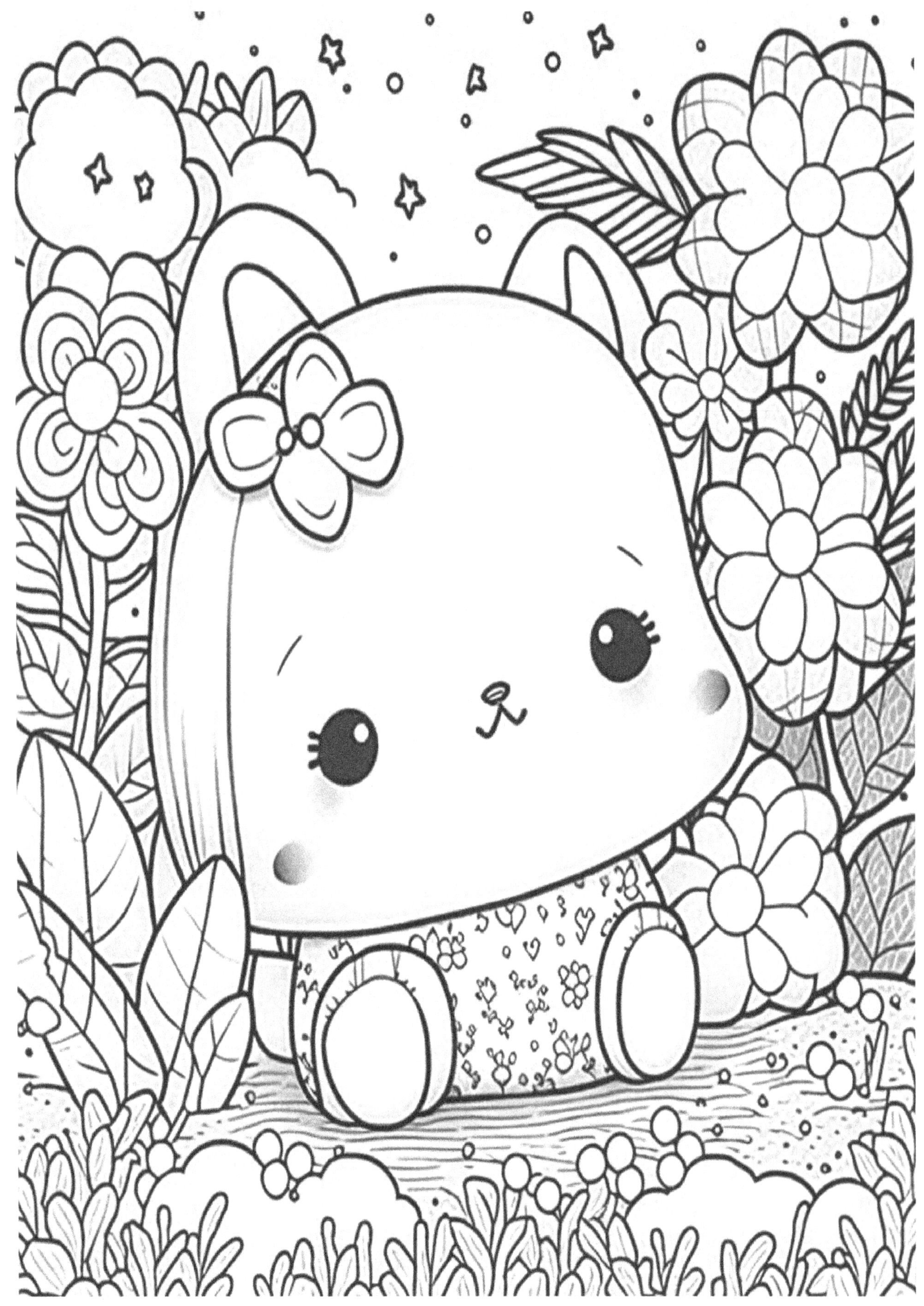

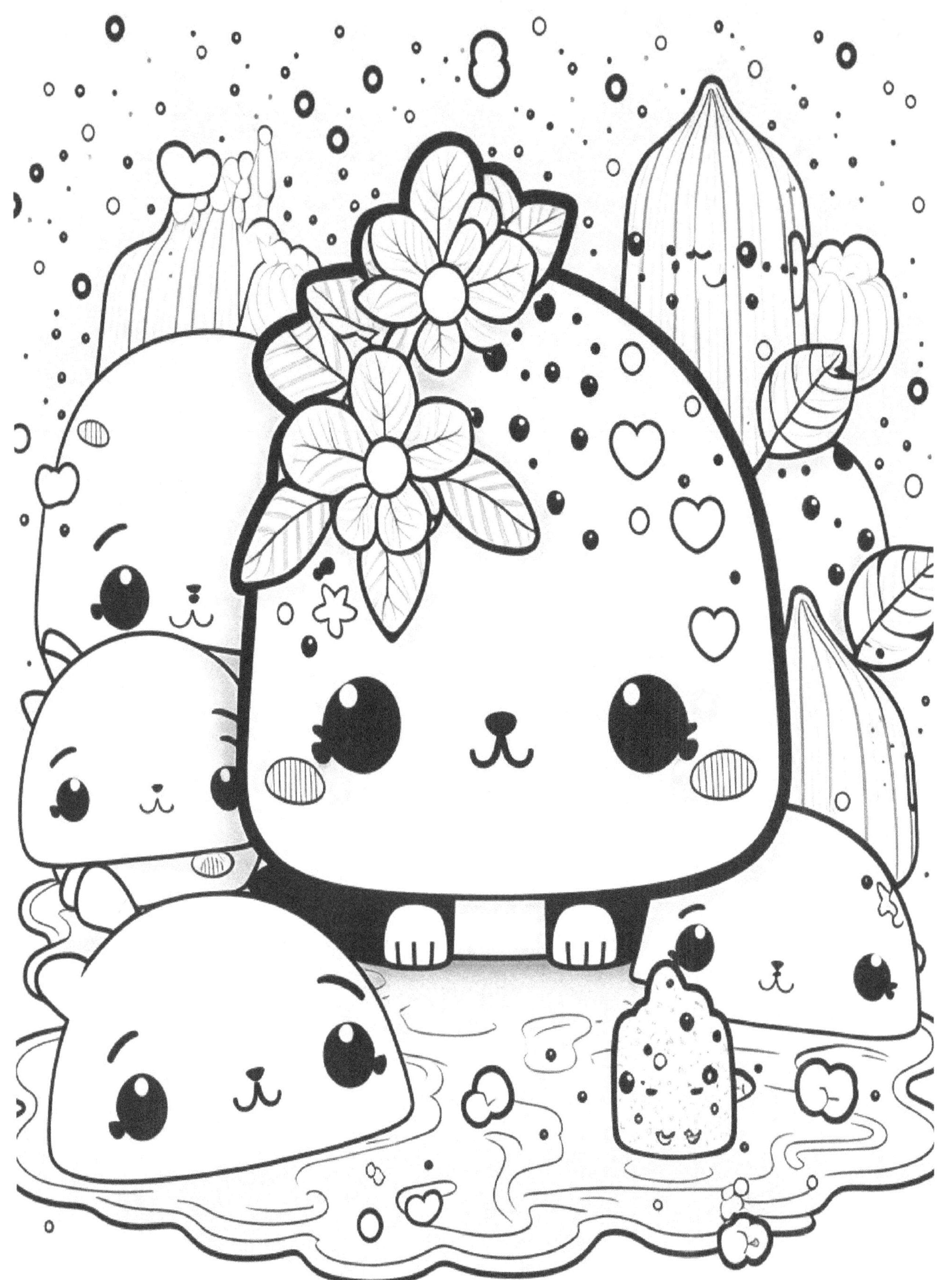

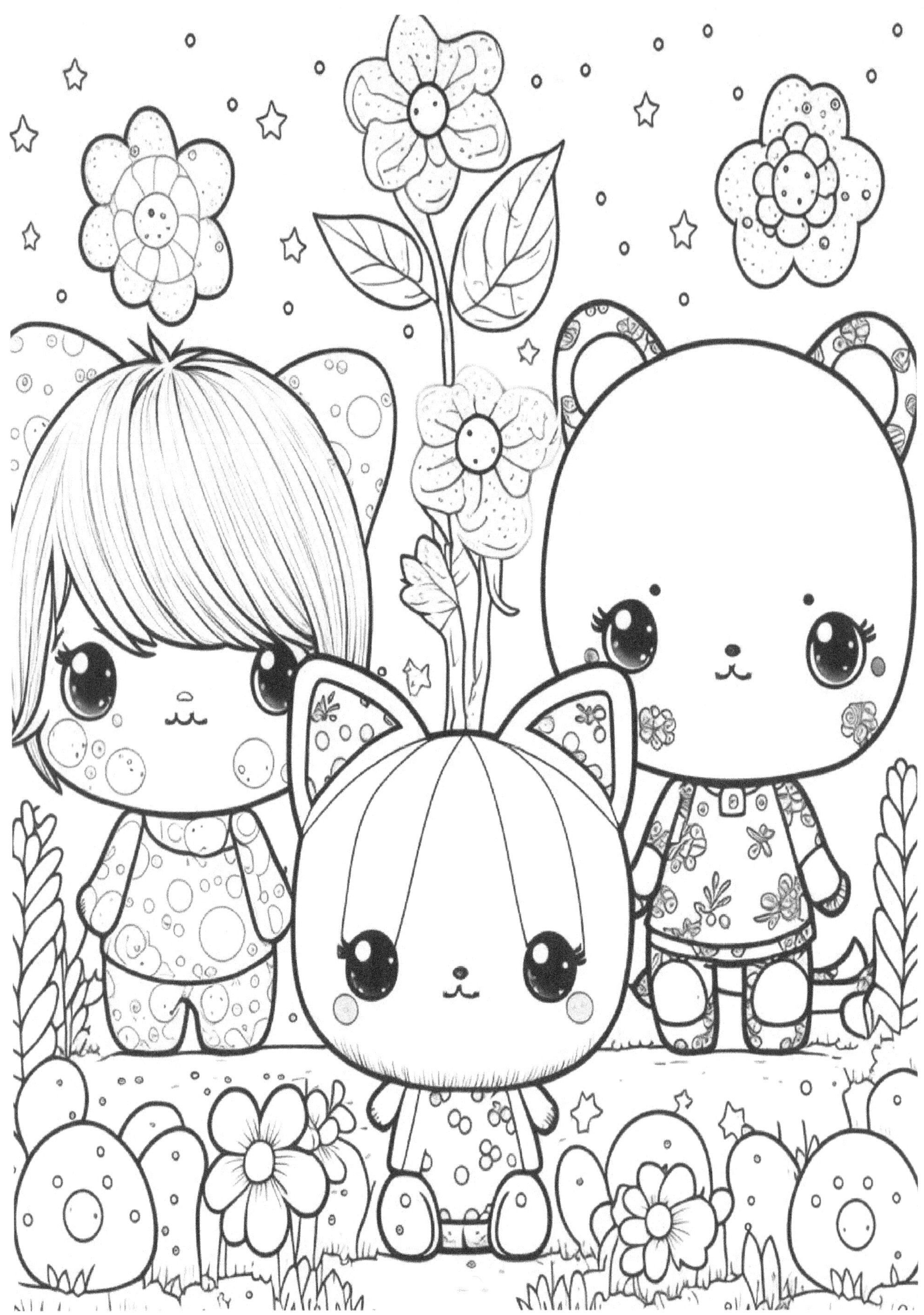

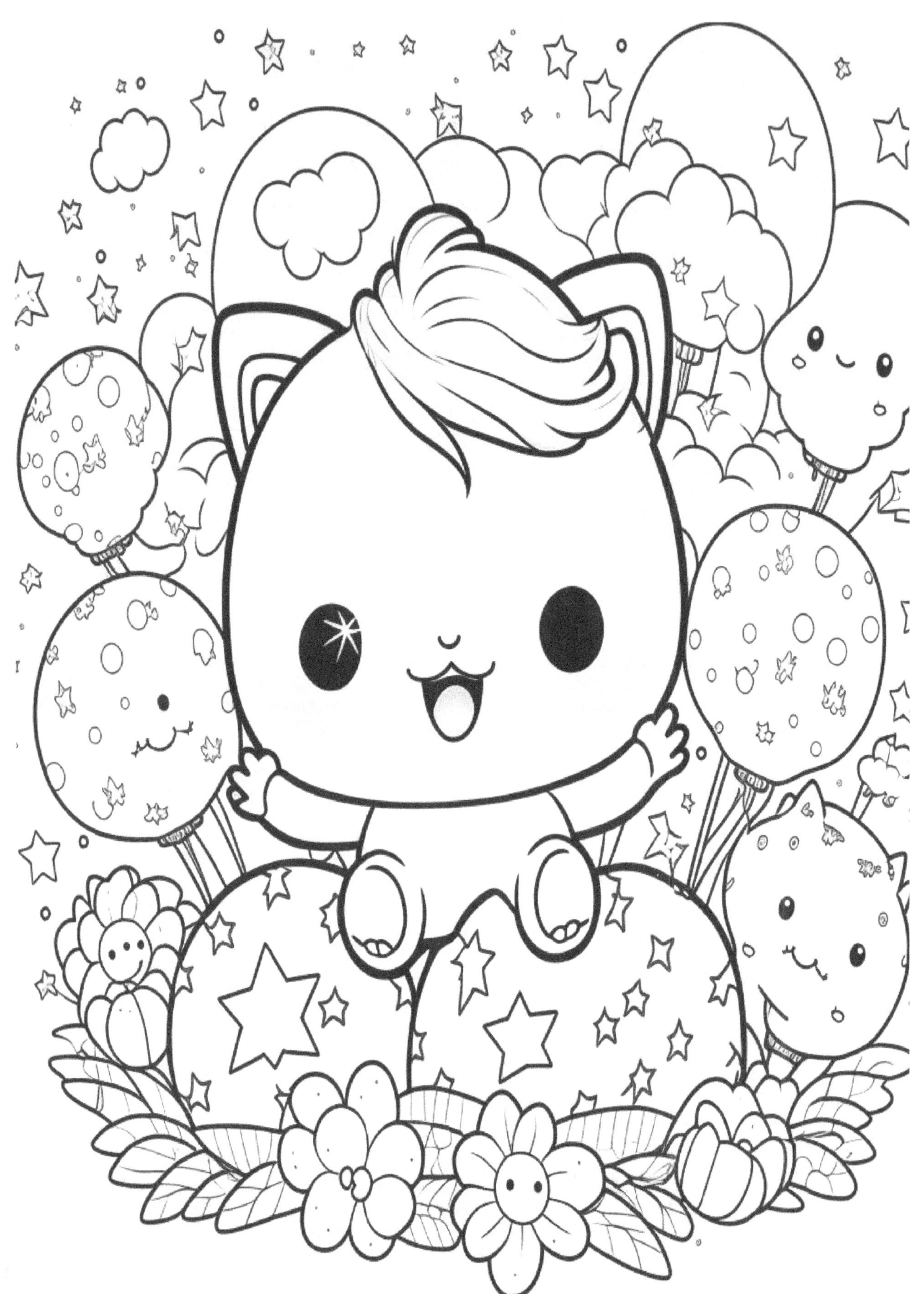